Enabling Grace

Langham
GLOBAL LIBRARY

This is no ordinary book. Grounded in biblical expertise and drawing from her long experience of and deep commitment to children with special needs, Dr. Susan Mathew develops a fresh approach to disability out of Paul's astounding theology of grace in weakness. The result is profound, moving, and truly extraordinary.

John M. G. Barclay, PhD
Lightfoot Professor of Divinity,
Durham University, UK

Having in her prior scholarship given voice to women as a South Asian Pentecostal New Testament/Pauline scholar, Susan Mathew now bears witness in the power of the Holy Spirit to the redemptive power of God in and through bodily impairment and disability, also out of the experience of being a mother to a son with cerebral palsy. Here we find exegesis, theological reflection, testimony, and practical ministerial exhortation brought together to show how the God of the Bible is on the side of those who are weaker and more vulnerable in society.

Amos Yong, PhD
Professor of Theology and Mission,
Fuller Theological Seminary, California, USA

I was delighted to peruse this scholarly work entitled *Enabling Grace: Towards Pauline Perspectives on Disability* written by Dr. Susan Mathew. This unique scholarly work is an in-depth study on issues related to disability from a Pauline perspective based on Corinthian correspondences.

The author proposes some basic principles for how to take care of a person with certain disability needs, a traumatic issue for some families today.

It is with immense joy and pleasure that I endorse this volume for the glory of God. This work will be a great resource to theological seminaries and churches as an eye-opening treatise on how to minister to those who are mainly neglected and marginalized in our communities.

B. Varghese, DTh
Principal Emeritus and Professor of New Testament Studies,
Faith Theological Seminary, Adoor, India

Dr. Susan Mathew's book is replete with biblical exegesis, theological insights, social realities, contextual implications, and personal reflections. She has traversed the otherwise intransigent strictures of traditional biblical hermeneutics to explore the area of disability in Judaism, the Greco-Roman world, Pauline framework, contemporary living, and her own first hand experiences. It is a work that deals with the subtleties of God's enabling grace in human weaknesses and disabilities. I highly recommend this unique, eye-opening, and helpful work.

Johnson Thomaskutty, PhD
Professor of New Testament,
United Theological College, Bengaluru, India

Enabling Grace

Towards Pauline Perspectives on Disability

Susan Mathew

GLOBAL LIBRARY

© 2025 Susan Mathew

Published 2025 by Langham Global Library
An imprint of Langham Publishing
www.langhampublishing.org

Langham Publishing and its imprints are a ministry of Langham Partnership

Langham Partnership
PO Box 296, Carlisle, Cumbria, CA3 9WZ, UK
www.langham.org

ISBNs:
978-1-83973-278-2 Print
978-1-78641-202-7 ePub
978-1-78641-203-4 PDF

Susan Mathew has asserted her right under the Copyright, Designs and Patents Act, 1988 to be identified as the Author of this work.

All rights reserved. No part of this publication may be reproduced, stored in a retrieval system or transmitted, in any form or by any means, electronic, mechanical, photocopying, recording or otherwise, without the prior written permission of the publisher or the Copyright Licensing Agency.

Requests to reuse content from Langham Publishing are processed through PLSclear. Please visit www.plsclear.com to complete your request.

All Scripture quotations, unless otherwise indicated, are taken from the New Revised Standard Version Bible, copyright © 1989 National Council of the Churches of Christ in the United States of America. Used by permission. All rights reserved.

Scripture quotations marked (NIV) are taken from the Holy Bible, New International Version®, NIV®. Copyright © 1973, 1978, 1984, 2011 by Biblica, Inc.™ Used by permission of Zondervan.

British Library Cataloguing-in-Publication Data
A catalogue record for this book is available from the British Library

ISBN: 978-1-83973-278-2

Cover & Book Design: projectluz.com

Langham Partnership actively supports theological dialogue and an author's right to publish but does not necessarily endorse the views and opinions set forth here or in works referenced within this publication, nor can we guarantee technical and grammatical correctness. Langham Partnership does not accept any responsibility or liability to persons or property as a consequence of the reading, use or interpretation of its published content.

To
Jyothish Koshy Mathew, our special gift from God,
and all specially abled children,

Soli Deo Gloria

Contents

Foreword xi
Acknowledgements xiii
Introduction 1
1 Issues on Disability.. 5
2 Disability in Antiquity.................................... 23
3 The Identity of the Weak in 1 Corinthians 37
4 The Person with Disability in the Body of Christ 51
5 Comfort in Affliction and Power in Weakness 81
6 From Brokenness to Blessing 103
7 Enabling Grace: Towards a Holistic Vision 117
   Bibliography 129

Foreword

The seeds of *Enabling Grace* were planted in 2003, the year Susan and I became parents to Jyothish, our son born with special needs. His arrival marked a definite turning point in our lives, profoundly impacting not only our family but also our Christian ministry. It was a journey we had neither foreseen nor felt equipped to take. Yet, by God's providence, we were gently drawn into the world of disability – a world filled with unique challenges, yet no less beautiful than what is often considered as "normal."

Like many parents of children with disabilities, we experienced an initial period of shock and questioning – "Why our child? Why us?" – followed by the overwhelming task of understanding how best to care for a child who was entirely dependent on us. This was compounded by our responsibilities toward our older children, and our academic and ministerial commitments at Faith Theological Seminary in Kerala, India.

It did not take long for us to realize that we could not move forward without God's sustaining grace. Through Jyothish, God gave us a new lens through which to see life: the fragile beauty and inherent giftedness of each moment, especially the developmental milestones that are often taken for granted. In the midst of our struggles, God began to teach us profound lessons. I remember one particularly difficult season when Jyothish was delayed in reaching certain milestones. As I poured out my anguish in prayer, I asked God, "Why have you wounded us like this?" In the stillness, I heard a quiet voice say, "You are called to heal the wounds of many. That's why I've given you this wound."

That moment marked the beginning of a deeper realization – of God's purpose for our child, and for our ministry: to be bearers of his light to others navigating similar darkness, to those marginalized and stigmatized by disability, affirming they are not alone – God is with them.

As we look back over the years – starting with Jyothish's birth in 2003, Susan's doctoral studies at Durham University from 2006 to 2010, our time in the UK, and the publication of her first book, *Women in the Greetings of Romans 16:1–16: A Study of Mutuality and Women's Ministry in the Letter to Romans* – we see a pattern of divine orchestration. In 2009, we initiated a small centre for children with special needs in our locality, which has since grown into Deepti Special School which now serves more than two hundred children and young adults with special needs, offering holistic care to them and support their families. Every stage of this journey, from its inception, has been a clear testament to God's grace.

In time, Susan began teaching a course on theology of disability to undergraduates at the seminary, while I did the same for postgraduate students. When she shared her desire to write a book on disability – drawing from her expertise in Pauline studies, our shared experience as parents, caregivers, and theological educators – I suggested the title *Enabling Grace*, and she embraced it. She later had an initial consultation with Prof. John M. G. Barclay, her PhD supervisor at Durham, whose encouragement and insights further strengthened her resolve.

Enabling Grace is far from an ivory tower theology. Rather, it's a theology forged in the crucible of suffering, born from the lived experience of pain and hope. It affirms the presence of a God who suffers with us and empowers us through his grace. Engaging Pauline reflections on grace and gift in conversation with the life experiences of people with disabilities, this book seeks to reimagine and reshape theological thought and practice. Its aim is to challenge discriminatory and exclusionary attitudes and ensure that theology neither marginalizes nor overlooks people with disabilities, but embraces disability as part of the broader human condition.

A huge congratulations to Susan Mathew, my beloved partner in both life and ministry, for her profound dedication in writing *Enabling Grace*. It is truly inspiring how she managed to complete this book amidst her demanding roles as a mother, theological educator, caregiver, and social entrepreneur. I'm confident that *Enabling Grace* will serve as a vital resource in disability theology, guiding readers who encounter challenges to experience grace in their suffering and discover hope in God's ultimate plans for their lives.

Rev. Mathew C. Varghese, PhD
Department of Theology and Ethics,
Faith Theological Seminary, Kerala, India

Acknowledgements

This work is the culmination of much effort and would not have been possible without the invaluable support, encouragement, and insights from many individuals and institutions.

I am profoundly grateful to Langham Partnership for their exceptional support, which enabled me to be a visiting academic researcher to the UK during two enriching periods – August to October 2015 and again in September 2017. I owe special thanks to Dr. Ian Shaw, then Scholars Director, and Elizabeth Hitchcock, Executive Assistant, whose support made my research journey smooth and deeply enriching. I am equally thankful to Mark Arnold, Editorial and Contracts Coordinator at Langham Literature, for his tireless efforts in facilitating the publication process and helping this work reach a wider audience.

A warm word of thanks goes to Ms. Liz McGregor for her kind visit in Cambridge – her gesture of personal connection and encouragement came at a meaningful time during my research.

The resources available at the Trinity College Library, Bristol, were invaluable, significantly enriching my study through their depth and scope. I am also thankful to the trustees of Hodgkin House, Bristol – especially Ronald Roberts, Chair of Trustees – for providing comfortable and convenient accommodation arranged by Langham, which offered the ideal environment for concentrated work.

I am especially indebted to Dr. Roy McCloughry, National Disability Adviser for the Archbishop's Council, Church of England. His generous sharing of insights, sustained mentorship, and provision of an extensive bibliography were foundational to shaping key themes of this work.

I extend heartfelt thanks to Prof. John M. G. Barclay, Lightfoot Professor of Divinity, Durham University and my PhD supervisor, for his enduring encouragement and support, which motivated and strengthened my academic pursuit.

To our precious special children, their parents and staff at Deepti Special School, your stories, resilience, and insight have deeply informed and energized many aspects of this study.

To the staff and students of Faith Theological Seminary, Kerala, India, thank you for cultivating an atmosphere of academic curiosity and vibrant community life.

My deepest gratitude goes to my parents for their ceaseless prayers, unwavering support, and encouragement, which have sustained me throughout this journey.

Finally, and most dearly, to my beloved husband Mathew and our wonderful children – your love, profound patience, sacrifice, and unfailing support provided the very foundation for this undertaking. Your love has been my greatest strength, and this work would not have been possible without you.

Above all, along with the Apostle Paul, I want to glorify God, for his all his wonderful works: "Praise be to the God and Father of our Lord Jesus Christ, the Father of compassion and the God of all comfort, who comforts us in all our troubles, so that we can comfort those in any trouble with the comfort we ourselves receive from God" (2 Cor 1:3-4, NIV).

Introduction

This book explores the theme of disability, emphasizing the enabling and transformative power of grace in the lives of persons with disabilities. My primary inspirations for writing this book are my own experiences as a mother of a child with special needs and my involvement in the ministry of support, care, and empowerment for children with special needs and their families in our local community.

My son, Jyothish, has been living with cerebral palsy (CP) for twenty-two years. In addition to caring for Jyothish, our family supports a large group of individuals with various disabilities, including cerebral palsy, autism, Down syndrome, intellectual disability, attention deficit hyperactivity disorder (ADHD), learning difficulties, visual impairment, and hearing impairment. These conditions range from mild to severe and affect individuals from different religious backgrounds.

I write from the perspectives of a parent, a Christian minister and a theological educator who is navigating the challenges and responsibilities of raising a differently-abled child.

Jyothish was the motivation behind the beginning of Deepti Special School and Rehabilitation Centre in our hometown in Kerala, India, to support families of children with special needs. At the School, we have children below four years old, students who are four to eighteen years old, and young adults who are over eighteen years old (these receive vocational training and instruction in life skills). The Centre provides services to people with disability whose ages range between one and forty years. More than 180 children are enrolled at the School and the Rehabilitation Centre. The services available at the Centre are: special education, creative play, physiotherapy, occupational therapy, speech therapy, hydrotherapy, music therapy, behaviour therapy, sensory integration, and early intervention with specific therapies. Those enrolled at the Centre work to improve their learning capacities, physical strength, coordination of muscles, skills required in their everyday life, and language and communication abilities. Furthermore, the Centre provides training in sports, music, and also other extracurricular activities.

In India, disability is understood in various ways, each with some cultural and religious underpinning. Understandings range from disability as: a curse, the result of demonic influence, being caused by a bad horoscope, and the outcome of bad karma in a previous life. Furthermore, there is a social stigma attached to the experience of disability, which applies across many religious traditions. Additional challenges for families are: the cost of the therapy and treatment they are required to pay, creating an obstacle to obtaining care for their disabled children; psychological pressures on parents including the disappointment of having a child with special needs; and the difficulty in accepting themselves as parents of a child with disabilities. Unfortunately, services for persons with disabilities are minimal and the support systems for them are not as developed as in high-income countries.

I know cases where parents have had to give up their jobs to look after their child (in some cases more than one child) with special needs. In those cases, one may ask: who will supply them with the money they need for food and their day-to-day expenses? At this point, we may appreciate the role of a health visitor[1] who can visit their homes, assess their needs, and inform other specialists who could help them. An effective support system in the early years of development might also include a network of families in similar conditions who come together and share their experiences and views. Such supports can relieve parents' psychological pressures, help them realize there are people who are undergoing equal or even worse problems, and, by mutually supporting and loving each other, give them the strength to move forward. Therefore, personal courage and strong powers of decision-making, together with communal support and acceptance, are of paramount importance in the context of families and people with disabilities.

In this book, I engage with selected Pauline letters and show the importance of both the communal and personal aspects of life in a disability context, and how the terminology of weakness in Paul can be interpreted in a context of disability. The first chapter deals with definitions, models and issues regarding disability. The second chapter deals with the background of this study, namely, disability in antiquity, in Judaism, and the Greco–Roman world. The third chapter deals with Paul's first epistle to the Corinthians and the identity of the weak in this epistle. It discusses the cross as the foundation regarding wisdom and folly, how status is reversed in the kingdom of God and implications for the person with disability (1 Cor 1:18–2:7). The fourth chapter considers the

---

1. In the United Kingdom (UK), a health visitor is a qualified nurse or midwife who has had extra training to help parents, families, and new babies stay healthy. Health visitors can visit people's homes or see parents and children at a child health clinic, GP surgery, or health centre. Health visitors' services are free to parents and are provided until a baby turns two years of age. The system in India is not as developed as in higher-income countries, such as the UK.

person with disability in the body of Christ. It begins with a discussion of the diversity of spiritual gifts and how the talents of the person with disability can be welcomed (1 Cor 12:4–11). It then examines the body of Christ in order to identify the place and role of persons with disability in the body of Christ, the diversity of members, and the task of honouring weaker members in the body of Christ (1 Cor 12:12–31). The third section emphasizes the greater gift – love – as it encompasses weakness (1 Cor 13) while the final section focuses on eschatology, and the place of the person with disability in the resurrection (1 Cor 15:35–58). The fifth chapter of this book focuses on 2 Corinthians, analyzing two sections of that letter. The first section considers mutuality and comfort in affliction (2 Cor 1:3–10); the second considers grace and power in weakness (2 Cor 12:7–10).

The sixth chapter deals with my personal story of having a child with special needs. It deals with the personal question of whether a child with cerebral palsy is a gift from God. It is the story of a family that faced unexpected problems due to the birth of a child with disability, how the family coped (and is coping) with it, and how that story turned into a community endeavour to change the lives of children with disability by supporting their families – people who have very limited resources and facilities to bring their children up.

The final chapter points to the significance of God's enabling grace and moves towards a holistic vision of grace in the context of affliction and disability. What were the benefits of Paul having a thorn in the flesh in his theology and mission? How much did this change his perspectives? The enabling in suffering is unique and the power of enabling grace is known in weakness. This points to a further significant aspect in enabling grace: the importance of mutual response and responsibility in the family, society, and church towards a person with disability.

1

Issues on Disability

Defining Disability

Disability is an umbrella term, covering impairments, activity limitations, and participation restrictions. Impairment is a problem in body function or structure; an *activity limitation* is a difficulty encountered by an individual in executing a task or action; while a *participation restriction* is a problem experienced by an individual in involvement in life situations. Thus disability is a complex phenomenon, reflecting an interaction between features of a person's body and features of the society in which he or she lives.[1]

It is to be noted that an impairment does not necessarily result in a disability. For instance, a person with hearing impairment might experience it as disability, if there is no provision to interpret a speech into sign language. Thus, a sensory deficit is called impairment. The term disability refers to functional limitations that result from a combination of impairment plus social environment.[2]

Disability has no discrimination as it's a universal reality that affects people irrespective of caste, class, colour, creed, culture and sex. Disability has been called an "open minority" because it is a group that most of us will "join" at some point of in our life.[3] As Elizabeth Stuarts notes, "The contrast is not

---

1. https://www.afro.who.int/health-topics/disabilities accessed on 6 June 2024.
2. Samuel George, "Persons with Disabilities in India," in *Doing Theology from Disability Perspective*. Edited by Wati Longchar and Gordon Cowans (Manila: ATESEA, 2011), 32.
3. Lennard J. Davis, *Enforcing Normalcy: Disability, Deafness, and the Body* (London: Verso, 1995), 1, cited by Deborah Beth Creamer, *Disability and Christian Theology: Embodied Limits and Constructive Possibilities* (New York: Oxford University, 2009), 18.

between the able and disabled but between temporarily able and disabled."⁴ Recognition of this fluidity, as Creamer points out, can be valuable in expanding our perspectives and breaking down some of the dichotomy between able and disabled and discrimination on the basis of disability. However, it should not lead to a sort of trivialization of disability or to minimize the legitimate justice concerns of people with disabilities.⁵

A Brief Review of UN Advocacy of Disability Issues

According to WHO an estimated 1.3 billion people experience significant disability. This represents 16 percent of the world's population, or 1 in 6 of us.⁶ "People with disabilities are the poorest of the poor; they are also the world's most powerless people, with women with disabilities being the most powerless group of all."⁷ Children with disabilities in low-income countries typically lack education and also lack proper care and life-support such as wheelchairs, proper medical aid, supportive therapy, etc. In such a situation, we have to think about empowerment, human rights, and advocacy. The quality of life of people with disabilities needs to be improved: it is possible to do that by changing oppressive attitudes towards them and changing social structures through giving them the same sets of opportunities as others have, regardless of their disability. As McCloughry and Morris rightly put it, "Their attitudes, gifts and opportunities are very different from one another, yet what they need is an opportunity to be themselves and to live life to the full alongside others."⁸ *The Universal Declaration of Human Rights* states that each person has "the right to security in the event of unemployment, sickness, disability, widowhood, old age, or lack of livelihood in circumstances beyond his control."⁹ Subsequent to

---

4. Lennard J. Davis, *Bending Over Backwards: Disability, Dismodernism and Other Difficult Positions* (New York: New York University, 2002), 25, cited by Creamer, *Disability and Christian Theology*, 18.

5. Creamer, *Disability and Christian Theology*, 18.

6. https://www.who.int/en/news-room/fact-sheets/detail/disability-and-health accessed on 25 July 2024. However, the earlier statistics presented in *World Report on Disability* by WHO indicates the prevalence of disability as 15 percent of global population. See, *World Report on Disability* (World Health Organization, 2011), 29.

7. Roy McCloughry and Wayne Morris, *Making a World of Difference: Christian Reflections on Disability* (London: SPCK, 2002), 1.

8. McCloughry, *Making a World of Difference*, 5.

9. https://www.un.org/sites/un2.un.org/files/2021/03/udhr.pdf. *Universal Declaration of Human Rights*, Article 25/1 (General Assembly of the United Nations in 1948) accessed on 4 July 2024.

the Declaration, international agencies such as the World Health Organization (WHO), the United Nations Children's Fund (UNICEF), and the International Labour Office (ILO) have worked together to develop human rights for people with disability and to promote anti-discrimination policies. Policies and declarations of the rights and needs of people with disability began to be developed from 1950 onwards and disability began to be a human rights issue rather than a medical issue. A range of international documents have highlighted that disability is a human rights issue, including the *World Programme of Action Concerning Disabled People* (1982), the *Convention on the Rights of the Child* (1989), and the *Standard Rules on the Equalisation of Opportunities for People with Disabilities* (1993). The Convention on the Rights of Persons with Disabilities (CRPD) is an international human rights convention which sets out the fundamental human rights of people with disability. CRPD – the most recent, and the most extensive recognition of the human rights of persons with disabilities – outlines the civil, cultural, political, social, and economic rights of persons with disabilities. Its purpose is to "promote, protect, and ensure the full and equal enjoyment of all human rights and fundamental freedoms by people with disabilities and to promote respect for their inherent dignity"[10] "It is not about deficiency, but about difference; and just as people from different ethnic backgrounds need their human rights promoted so do disabled people."[11] The year 1981 was declared as the International Year of Disabled Persons (IYDP) by the UN General Assembly in 1976 to heighten focus on the need for people with disability to be fully integrated into society. Subsequently, the World Programme of Action Concerning Disabled Persons came into being focussing on three areas: prevention (preventing disability from occurring), rehabilitation (promoting the right to effective rehabilitation), and equalisation of opportunities (full participation of people with disability in their communities as citizens).

Afterwards, the United Nations Decade of Disabled Persons (1983–92) came into being. In 1993, the United Nations published the *Standard Rules on Equalization of Opportunities for Persons with Disabilities*[12] setting out norms by which governments could cooperate with legislation that would ensure that people with disability throughout the world could enjoy full participa-

---

10. *World Report on Disability* (World Health Organization, 2011), 9.

11. McCloughry, *Making a World of Difference*, 6.

12. Among the major outcomes of the Decade of Disabled Persons was the adoption, by the General Assembly, of the *Standard Rules on the Equalization of Opportunities for Persons with Disabilities* in 1993, https://www.un.org/esa/socdev/enable/dissre00.html accessed on 17 July 2024.

tion in society as citizens. There was also increasing focus, within the UN, on the special problems faced by women with disabilities and children with disabilities, and on the challenges posed by wars throughout the world. The WHO worked towards eradicating poliomyelitis, recognizing it as one of the major causes for disability. Regardless of all the developments in the area of disability, low-income countries still have a long way to go towards adequacy of provision in resources and trained staff for disabled people.

Disability in India

As per Census 2011, in India, out of the 121 Cr (1.21 billion) population, about 2.68 Cr (26. 8 million) persons are "disabled" which is 2.21 percent of the total population.[13] Among the disabled population 56 percent (1.5 Cr/15 million) are males and 44 percent (1.18 Cr/11.8 million) are females. In the total population, the male and female population is 51 percent and 49 percent respectively. The majority (69 percent) of the disabled population resided in rural areas (1.86 Cr/18.6 million) while 0.81 Cr/8.1 million live in urban areas. In the case of total population also, 69 percent are from rural areas while the remaining 31 percent resided in urban areas.[14] However, a study based on the most recent National Family Health Survey 2019–21 (NFHS-5)[15] gives a more realistic data of overall prevalence of disability in India as 4.5 percent.[16]

One can decipher the condition of people with disability in India by seeing the majority of its huge population living below the poverty line. In rural areas, people with disabilities often live in very challenging conditions, with many having to rely on begging to survive.[17] Several factors contribute to the difficulties they face, including limited access to healthcare, education, and employment opportunities. Additionally, societal attitudes and lack of infrastructure can exacerbate their struggles.

---

13. "Disabled People in India: A Statistical Profile," 18. https://niepmd.tn.nic.in/documents/Disabledpersons2016_2408.pdf accessed on 7 July 2024.

14. "Disabled People in India: A Statistical Profile," 18.

15. https://main.mohfw.gov.in/sites/default/files/NFHS-5_Phase-II_0.pdf accessed on 20 July 2024.

16. Sweta Pattnaik , Jogesh Murmu , Ritik Agrawal, et al., "Prevalence, pattern and determinants of disabilities in India: Insights from NFHS-5 (2019–21)," Frontiers in Public Health, https://www.frontiersin.org/journals/public-health/articles/10.3389/fpubh.2023.1036499/full, accessed on 7 July 2024.

17. Samuel George, "Persons with Disabilities in India," 34.

Several factors contribute to the difficulties they face, including limited access to healthcare, education, and employment opportunities. Additionally, societal attitudes and lack of infrastructure can exacerbate their struggles. The situations in urban setting are not better either for people with disabilities. Persons with disabilities often place significant economic and emotional burdens on their parents and guardians. Above all people with disability often have to bear the brunt of the social stigmatization in India. Disabled people might be feared and discriminated against as evil, as cursed and spiritually afflicted.[18] Treatment and training may be perceived as defiance of God's will or interference with a person's *karma*, reinforcing the belief that a disability is a result of misdeeds in one's past life. This is the predicament of people with disabilities: they are marginalized by society and constrained by religious beliefs.

A discussion on disability in India cannot overlook the pervasive influence of caste, patriarchy, and gender, and their implications for women with disabilities. They must contend with caste prejudices, patriarchal norms, and discrimination. Often, they are the poorest and most stigmatized, marginalized, and oppressed individuals in developing nations. Their plight is aptly captured in the words of Anita Ghai: "In a culture being a daughter is a curse, being a diasabled daughter is a fate worse than death."[19]

Nevertheless, in recent years, there have been perceptible positive changes in societal perceptions of persons with disabilities. Thanks to government initiatives and persistent efforts by NGOs, it is now recognized that most persons with disabilities can lead better lives if provided with equal opportunities and effective access to rehabilitation measures.

Models of Disability

Disability is perceived differently depending on various models. Prominent among them are the medical model or functional limitation model and social or minority group model. There are also other models such as tragedy/charity model, moral and affirmation model.

---

18. Susan Erb and Barbara Harris-White, *Outcast from Social Welfare: Adult Disability, Incapacity and Development in Rural South India* (Bangalore: Books for Change, 2002), 9.

19. Anita Ghai, "Disabled Women: An Excluded Agenda of Indian Feminism" in *Hypatia* 17(3): 53, cited by Amos Yong, *Theology and Down Syndrome*, 118.

Medical Model or Functional Limitation Model

In the medical model, the focus is on what one cannot physically or functionally do. It claims that the disabled person's functional ability deviates from that of the normal human body.[20] Under the medical model, disabled people are defined by their illness or medical condition. The medical model regards disability as an individual problem. It promotes the view of a disabled person as dependent and needing to be cured or cared for, and justifies the way in which disabled people have been systematically excluded from society. The disabled person is the problem, not society. Control resides firmly with professionals; choices for the individual are limited to the options provided and approved by the "helping" expert.

Positively, the medical model aims at improving the quality of life of persons with disability, by increasing the functionality to allow them to lead a more "normal life." Additionally, modern medical technology provides assistive devices/helps that are beneficial to people with disability to a great extent.

Nevertheless, the medical model is unwelcomed by the disabled community because it focuses on impairments or illnesses, defining individuals based on these conditions. It categorizes disabled people as abnormal, leading to their disenfranchisement from society. This model does not require society to change its exclusive practices or attitudinal barriers.

Social or Minority Group Model

The social model of disability sees the issue of "disability" as a socially created problem and a proper response as requiring the full integration of individuals into society. In this model, individuals are considered disabled insofar as they experience prejudice and exclusion.[21] Disability is not an attribute of an individual, but rather a complex collection of conditions, many of which are created by the social environment. According to the social model, "to be disabled means to be discriminated against."[22] There is a shift from the medical model, which saw the person with disability as a patient with a problem, to seeing the person with disability as a citizen with rights.

Hence, the management of the problem requires social action, and it is the collective responsibility of society at large to make the environmental

---

20. Creamer, *Disability and Christian Theology*, 23.
21. Creamer, *Disability and Christian Theology*, 25.
22. Len Barton, ed., *Disability and Society: Emerging Issues and Insights* (New York: Longman, 1996), 13.

modifications necessary for the full participation of people with disabilities in all areas of social life. The issue is both cultural and ideological, requiring individual, community, and large-scale social change. From this perspective, equal access for someone with an impairment/disability is a human rights issue of major concern.

The following table compares the medical model and the social model.[23]

Table 1. Comparison of Medical and Social Models of Disability

The Medical Model	The Social Model
Locates disability in the individual	Locates disability in the society
Focuses on the individual's need to adjust to society	Focuses on the need of society to adjust to the need of the individual
People as patients	People as citizens
Disability as deficit	Disability as diversity
Prioritizes cure	Prioritizes social change
Disability as professionally defined	Disability as self-defined
"This is my diagnosis"	"This is my life"
Uses science	Uses politics
Maintained by non-disabled people	Maintained by people with disabilities

The Tragedy/Charity Model

This depicts disabled people as victims of circumstances and therefore deserving of pity. The tragedy/charity model regards disabled people's lives as tragic victims only deserving of pity. Probably, the tragedy/charity model and medical model are the most commonly used models by non-disabled people to define and explain disability. The tragedy/charity model agrees with the medical model that disability is a problem that is inherited in the person who has fallen victim to it.

Out of tragedy and pity emerges a culture of "care." When concern and care for the disabled are promoted, critics contend that this approach is dis-

---

23. Roy McCloughry, *The Enabled Life: Christianity in a Disabling World* (London: SPCK, 2013), 23–34. See also https://journalsofindia.com/medical-model-of-disability-vs-social-model-of-disability/ accessed on 16 November 2015.

empowering and fosters considerable discrimination.[24] Numerous charities exist to support and care for people with specific disabilities, often leading to medical classification, segregation, and, as seen with the medical model, the institutionalization of many disabled individuals. People with disabilities should not be objects of pity or charity. They are persons with dignity. So steps need to be taken and funds to be channeled to promote the empowerment of disabled people and their full integration into society as equal citizens who require respect but not pity.

Religious/Moral Model of Disability

The moral model of disability argues that people are morally responsible for their own disability. For example, if congenital, the disability may be seen as a result of the bad actions of the person's parents, or as a result of practicing witchcraft.

The religious model views disability as a punishment inflicted upon an individual or family by an external force. It can be due to misdemeanors by the disabled person, someone in the family or community group, or forebears. In some cases, the disability stigmatizes a whole family, lowering their status or even leading to total social exclusion. Or, it can be interpreted as an individual's inability to conform within a family structure. Conversely, it can be seen as necessary afflictions to be suffered before some future spiritual reward. Furthermore, echoes of this can be seen in the doctrine of karma in Indian religions.[25]

The Affirmation Model

The affirmation model addresses the limitations of the social model through the realisation of positive identity which encompasses impairment as well as disability. The World Health Organization introduced *The International Classification of Functional Disability and Health (ICF)* in 2001 as a result of a consultation by sixty-five nations over seven years. "The focus is 'life' – how a person lives with and copes with their health condition and how they can be helped to live a more fruitful life. It has implications not only for medicine but

---

24. Kofi Amponsah-Bediako, "Relevance of Disability Models from the Perspective of a Developing Country: An Analysis," *Developing Country Studies* 3, no. 11, 2013: 124.

25. https://www.disabled-world.com/definitions/disability-models.php accessed on 16 November 2015.

also for law, social planning, environmental change, and human rights."[26] This model is characterized by activities and participation instead of disability and handicap. In this model, everybody is involved rather than just people with disability. I suggest that a holistic model is the most significant for the person with disability. It is essentially a non-tragic view of disability and impairment, grounded in the benefits of lifestyle and the life experience of being impaired and disabled.

An Appraisal of Disability in the Pauline Literature

There is a consensus among scholars that the apostle Paul suffered from some illness/disease, that he prayed three times for its removal while referring to it as a "thorn in the flesh" (2 Cor 12:7). Although there are different opinions regarding this "thorn," in Paul's epistles we come across terms that express his bodily weakness. Moreover, in the light of 1 and 2 Corinthians, it seems that Paul has a positive approach to suffering, affliction, and weakness, finding in it an opportunity for the infilling of God's power.

For many years, not much attention has been given to Paul's references to his sufferings amid his discussion of theology and his passing references to the persecution he experienced (Gal 4:14–20; 5:11; 6:12, 17). In Galatians 4:13, Paul says that he first preached the gospel to them "because of the weakness of the flesh." "You know that it was because of a physical infirmity that I first announced the gospel to you," Black argued that here "weakness" (*astheneia*) "refers to a physical condition of the apostle, and not to an unimpressive appearance, timidity, the emotional scars from persecution, sexual desires, human frailty in general, and some other figurative meaning."[27] Paul's weakness in Galatians is seen as a physical infirmity since he supplemented the term "weakness" with "in the flesh."

Such references may be directly relevant to the experience of those who are affected with disabilities/impairment, who are weak in the body in a way that affects their movements, growth, social life, spiritual life, their concept of God, their view of their own body, their identity, and their ongoing life, etc. We have to give attention to those people who are born with severe disabilities (physical and/or intellectual) and who have not been given a chance to live their life in its fullness. How does the concept of body, soul, and spirit apply in them?

---

26. McCloughry, *Making a World of Difference*, 21.
27. D. A. Black, "Weakness language in Galatians," *Grace Theological Journal* 4 (1983): 29.

The present work focuses on 2 Corinthians 12:7–10; it looks at the context in which Paul speaks about weakness, the sufficiency of grace, and the power that is made perfect in weakness.

The paradoxes of weakness and strength, and also foolishness and wisdom, are significant to Paul's discussion in Romans and 1 and 2 Corinthians. In his personal life, Paul suffered disability, which is described as "a thorn in the flesh" (2 Cor 12:7). The word "weak" (*asthenēs*), used in this context, may be considered equivalent to the modern term "disability." As Albl suggests, "Disability is not a peripheral or incidental topic in Paul's thought; rather it is one that brings us to the very heart of Paul's central beliefs about the human and divine."[28] Paul says that he was physically afflicted (Gal 4:13). There is here a paradox that the apostle who healed others was not healed himself.

This raises several pertinent questions:

- What is the nature of the disability that Paul suffered?
- Can "weak" (*asthenēs*) and its cognate noun "weakness" (*astheneia*) be taken in an inclusive way to signify disability?
- Does Paul use the paradox of weak and strong in line with his theology of the cross (*theologiacrucis*)?
- How does weakness/disability redefine grace in Paul's understanding?
- Paul does not present the notion of power in its conventional understanding, as autocratic, alienating, and dominating, but does speak about power in weakness. Is the expression "power in weakness" (2 Cor 12:9) a strong critique of the misuse/abuse of power in society?

The Social Setting of First Century Corinth

In order to understand Paul's use of weakness terminology, it is best to situate it in the context of Corinth, where individualism, status, self-display, and competition for honour prevailed.

---

28. Martin Albl, "For Whenever I am Weak, Then I am Strong: Disability in Paul's Epistles," in *This Abled Body: Rethinking Disabilities in Biblical Studies*, ed. by H. Avalos, S. J. Melcher and J. Schipper (Atlanta: SBL, 2007), 145. See also, McCloughry, *Making a World of Difference*, 15.

Individualism

The Greco-Roman context of the Hellenistic/early Roman era saw a rise of individualism and a decline of the city-state with its social bonds and corporate solidarity. People became more individualistic and appreciated the autonomy and self-sufficiency of the individual.[29] They focused on themselves and cultivated self-worth, self-appreciation, and self-glorification.[30]

Status

Rank determined one's behaviour, relationships, and legal privileges. People belonged to one of two social classes: either the "respectable" (*honestiores*), who possessed power and were esteemed for their *dignitas*, or the "insignificant" (*humuliores*), who lacked *dignitas* and had no honour in society.[31] Wealth determined the status of people: people worshipped wealth, and poverty was regarded with contempt.[32] One could obtain utmost social respectability through virtuous living, and the worth of name, occupation, neighbourhood, talent, education, religion, political office, or athletic accomplishment.[33] Wealth and status were cherished features in the urban life of the first century CE.

Self-Display

The Greeks regarded projection of status as important. "The rich flaunted their wealth, erecting monuments and buildings in their own honour and purchasing political office. The less fortunate were equally interested in self-glorification,

---

29. Frederick C. Grant, *Roman Hellenism and the New Testament* (New York: Charles Scribner's Sons, 1962), 15; J. Ferguson, *The Religions of the Roman Empire* (NewYork: Cornell University, 1970), 190; Timothy B. Savage, *Power through Weakness: Paul's Understanding of the Christian Ministry in 2 Corinthians*, SNTS Monograph Series (Cambridge: Cambridge University, 1996), 19.

30. For cultivating self-worth, see Seneca, *Epistles, Volume I: Epistles 1–65*, trans. Richard M. Gummere. LCL 75 (Cambridge: Harvard University, 1917), 34.3–4, 6.46, 115.3–4; Plutarch, *Moralia*, Harold North Fowler trans. 14 Vols. LCL (Cambridge: Harvard University, 1927), 76b–e. Although Stoics stressed duty to others, their ultimate goal was for individual virtue (see, for example, Cicero's *De Officiis*). M. Tullius Cicero, *De Officiis*, Eng. trans. Walter Miller (Cambridge: Harvard University, 1913), 1.4. "The entire ancient ethic is based on a pronounced feeling of self and worth in the individual man."

31. P. Garnsey, *Social Status and Legal Privilege in the Roman Empire* (Oxford: Clarendon, 1970), 221–80; M. I. Finley, The *Ancient Economy* (Berkeley: University of California, 1973), 87.

32. R. MacMullen, *Roman Social Relations* (London: Yale University, 1974), 109–10. Poverty was "evil and unfortunate" (Dio Chrysostom, *Orations* 7.115) and "a disgrace and a dishonour" (Cicerom, *Tusculan Disputations* 5–15).

33. Savage, *Power through Weakness*, 21, 22.

though their methods were simpler."[34] Privacy was uncommon in the cities and one's life was known to all.[35] In such circumstances, wealthy people were known for their riches and had public honour. On the other hand, the poor and their miseries brought contempt and ridicule.[36] *Doxa* (glory) became the ideal, and people looked for personal esteem, worth, and glory that brought public applause to themselves.

Competition for Honour

Competition for honour was pervasive in the first century CE. People tried to maintain their glory and improve their position in order to sustain and enhance their reputation. Competition for honour resulted in expressions of pride and arrogance, in boasting as an activity worthy of honour, and in indifference to the need of others. "The lowly had no self-respect, no public standing – "they were slaves on a low scale."[37] Consequently, division, conflict, and enmity afflicted the communities of the early empire.[38] The wealthy in Corinth paid large sums of money to erect monuments, gain honorific inscriptions, make donations for building funds, and give numerous benefactions to the city of Corinth. Self-display of power, wealth, and status were common among the elite, and even those on the lower parts of the social scale. As Savage puts it, "In Corinth, perhaps more than anything else, social ascent was the goal, boasting, and self-display the means, personal power and glory the reward."[39] Thus people paid high regard to public attention and applause that created pride and boasting, and measured others by criteria of status and wealth.

---

34. Savage, *Power through Weakness*, 22.

35. MacMullen, *Social Relations*, 62–64; W. A. Meeks, *The First Urban Christians: The Social World of the Apostle Paul* (New Haven and London: Yale University, 1983), 118.

36. Petronius, *Satyricon,* trans. Sarah Ruden (Indianapolis: Hackett, 2000), 57, and Juvenal, *Satire*, edited by A. S. Kine, 3.153–54.

37. Epictetus, *His Discourses*, in Four Books, trans. Thomas Wentworth Higginson (New York: Thomas Nelson and Sons, 1890), 4.1.55, cited by Savage, *Power through Weakness*, 24.

38. Dio Chrysostom, *Orations*, English trans. J. W. Cohoon (London: Heinemann, 1932), 38.24; Compare R. MacMullen, *Enemies of the Roman Order: Treason, Unrest, and Alienation in the Empire* (Cambridge: Harvard University, 1967), 94; Samuel Dill, *Roman Society in the Last Century of the Western Empire* (London: Macmillan, 1900), 375.

39. Savage, *Power through Weakness*, 41.

Survey of Weakness (*astheneia*) Terminology

The *asthenēs* wordgroup (the verb *astheneō*, the noun *astheneia*, and the adjective *asthenēs*) embraces the full range of physical, emotional, social, economic, and even spiritual incapacity. It stands in contrast to *sthenos* (strength), and so has the meaning of powerlessness, weakness, lack of strength, with some semantic overlap with sickness (*nosos*).[40]

In the Greek version of the Old Testament (LXX), the term is used to render a large number of Hebrew equivalents, however its use in the sense of sickness is very rarely found in the Old Testament; an example is Leah's weak eyes (Gen 29:17). It is variously also used to question whether the inhabitants of Canaan are strong (Num 13:19) and in relation to: disease (Dan 8:27; *nosos*); human weakness (Judg 16:7, 11, 17); the social significance of Gideon's family (Judg 6:15); political weakness (2 Sam 3:1). Other references are Jeremiah 6:21; 18:15, 23; Hosea 4:5; 5:5; Nahum 2:5; 3:3; Zephaniah 1:3 (a hindrance/stumbling block); Psalms 9:3; 27:2; 58:7; 107:12; compare Job 28:4 (stumbling of the ungodly and of enemies); and human poverty and wretchedness (Pss 6:2; 31:10; 88:9; 109:24; cf. Job 4:4; Prov 21:13; 22:22).

The root *asthen* appears eighty-three times in the New Testament. This wordgroup is used in its literal sense in the synoptic Gospels and in John, whereas the figurative sense, resulting from theological reflection, occurs in the Pauline literature. It has a general sense of weakness (1 Pet 3:7; 2 Cor 10:10; Matt 26:41; cf. Mk 14:38). The Gospels use the word in the specific sense of bodily weakness or sickness (Matt 10:8; Luke 13:11; Acts 9:37; John 4:46). In Paul, the wordgroup is used in reference to sin, to ethics, and to Christology.[41] Of its eighty-three uses in the New Testament, forty-four uses are in the Pauline epistles.

Three general observations can be made about this:

a. In Romans 6:19 "weakness of the flesh" refers to the natural weakness of a human being. Romans 8:26 is about human powerlessness and the need for the Spirit's power (*dunamis*). In 1 Corinthians 15:43 it is used to characterise the present human condition, ending in

---

40. H. G. Link, "Weakness" (ἀσθένεια) in Colin Brown, ed. *New Testament Theology vol. 3, Pri-Z* (Exeter: Paternoster, 1978), 993. It can also be used in a wider sense as the opposite of *dunamis* (power) or *ischuros* (strong) to express some sort of weakness, for example, the frailty of women, the weakness of human nature (Plato, *Laws* 854a) and of human life (Herodotus, *Histories*, trans. A. D. Godley, LCL (London: Heinnemann, 1920), 2, 47; 8, 51) but also to express economic weakness, that is, lack of influence, or poverty (Herodotus 2, 88).

41. W. Bauer, W. F. Arndt, F. W. Gingrich and F. W. Danker, *Greek–English Lexicon of the New Testament and Other Early Christian Literature* (London: University of Chicago, 2000), 142.

death, and in Romans 8:4 Paul develops the concept of weakness by bringing out its association with the law.

b. Paul points to *astheneia* as the sphere of impermanence in the created order, the powerlessness of the law, and human incapacity before God. But in a further line of thought, he finds here the place where God's might is exhibited. He unveils the theology of "the cross as the site of weakness" when he argues against his opponents in Corinth. In this context, Paul uses *astheneia* with reference to the suffering and death of Jesus Christ. Christ was crucified in weakness and in this Crucified One the weakness of God comes to light, which to human eyes appears to be mere folly and powerlessness (1 Cor 1:25, 27). God has demonstrated his might in weakness, that is, in the death of Christ, by raising him from the dead (2 Cor 13:4). Paul regards his own weakness as the opposition from opponents in Corinth, and he thinks that he has fellowship in Christ's sufferings (1 Cor 2:2; 4:10; 2 Cor 13:4). Furthermore, God's power is at work in weakness. Therefore, he would rather boast of his weakness (2 Cor 11:30; 12:5, 9–10; 13:9), for God's power is made perfect in weakness (2 Cor 12:9).[42] "Along the basic line of the New Testament paradox, weakness as a form of manifestation of the divine on earth is a mark of honour for a Christian."[43]

c. There is a third line of thought used by Paul in hortatory contexts, where he distinguishes between the strong (Rom 15:1) and the weak (Rom 14:1) in faith. In this context, weakness does not mean human powerlessness compared to God, or the sufferings of Christ and his disciples; rather, the direct use of the terms "strong" and "weak" represent catchwords or slogans used by the church in Corinth and Rome (1 Cor 8:10; Rom 14:1–15:13).

Within the Pauline epistles, *astheneia* and its cognates are most often used (around thirty-seven times) in Romans and the Corinthian letters.[44] The motif of weakness is developed in 2 Corinthians 10–13, where the words appear fourteen times; it is used fifteen times in 1 Corinthians and eight times in Romans.

---

42. Link, "Weakness," 995.

43. Stahlin, ἀσθένεια, *TDNT* 1, Gerhard Kittel (ed.), Geoffrey W. Bromiley (trans. and ed.) (Grand Rapids: Eerdmans, 1964), 490–93, at 491.

44. David Alan Black, *Paul, Apostle of Weakness: Astheneia and its Cognates in the Pauline Literature*, rev. ed. (Eugene: Pickwick, 2012), 7.

In the light of the extensive use of weakness terminology in 1–2 Corinthians, Black suggests that "it was primarily in the Corinthian correspondence that the Pauline idea of weakness developed."[45]

Paul's Perspective on Suffering

The writings of Paul the apostle make clear his perspective on suffering.[46] He embraced suffering or even death for the gospel.[47] It is plausible to assume that suffering was woven into his life and ministry. The epistles of Paul record different terms denoting the language of suffering. The terms used are:

1. *paschō, sumpaschō, pathēma* – general terms for the suffering of Paul and the churches (sixteen times)
2. *thlibō, thlipsis* – tribulation, affliction or distress (twenty-nine times)
3. *diōkō, diōgmos* – persecution (sixteen times), including Paul's former persecuting activities (1 Cor 15:9; Gal 1:13, 23; Phil 3:6)
4. *(sug)kakopatheō* – bear ill treatment, endure affliction (four times in 2 Timothy).

Many other related terms occur in Paul's catalogues of sufferings: seven terms in Romans 8:35 alone, eleven terms in 1 Corinthians 4:11–13, four contrastive pairs in 2 Corinthians 4:8–9, eighteen terms for hardships of various kinds occur in 2 Corinthians 6:4–5, 2 Corinthians 11:23–29 (where he lists twenty-seven experiences of hardship, especially various kinds of danger; compare 1 Cor 15:40), and in 2 Corinthians 12:10 five items are listed.[48]

Howell notes three purposes that empowered Paul in his suffering.[49] First, Paul endured suffering for the sake of the gospel of Christ and for the edification of the body of Christ (2 Tim 1:8, 12; 2:3, 9; 4:5). His afflictions are for

---

45. Black, *Paul, Apostle of Weakness*, 8.

46. The Acts 9 account of Paul's conversion describes his vision of the persecuted Christ and Paul's mission to suffer for Christ's sake (9:5, 16). Luke's account in Acts portrays the sufferings faced by Paul as he proceeds with his evangelistic mission in numerous locations: Damascus (Acts 9:23–25); Pisidian Antioch (13:45–46); Iconium (14:4–5); Lystra (14:19); Thessalonica (17:4–9); Berea (17:13); Corinth (18:6, 12–13); Greece (20:3); Jerusalem and Caesarea (21:27–36; 22:22–23; 23:2–4, 12–15; 25:9–12, 16–19; 26:21); and Rome (28:23–28). Paul also reminds the Galatians that they have to undergo hardships to enter into the kingdom of God (Acts 14:22).

47. Don N. Howell Jr., "Paul's Theology of Suffering," in eds. John Robert L. Plummer and John Mark Terry, *Paul's Missionary Methods: In His Time or Ours* (Leicester: Inter-Varsity Press, 2012), 96.

48. Howell, "Paul's Theology of Suffering," 97, note 5.

49. Howell, "Paul's Theology of Suffering," 97–101.

the comfort of the church, so that the Corinthians learn to patiently endure their sufferings (2 Cor 1:5–7; Eph 3:13). Paul willingly endures his physical sufferings because he fills up what is lacking in Christ's suffering (Col 1:24).

Second, suffering brings participation in the humiliation experienced by Jesus; giving up self-reliance and putting trust in Jesus releases the power of the risen Lord to be active in his life (2 Cor 1:5; 4:7–12). Suffering is a mark of the inheritance of the kingdom of God (2 Cor 4:16–18; Rom 8:17–18). "Between the 'with him' of the already ('buried with him') and the 'with him' of the not yet ('raised with him'), there is the 'with him' of the in-between times ('suffer with him')."[50] Paul observes that sufferings such as "weaknesses, insults, hardships, persecutions, and calamities" are useful to his personal spiritual life since they enable the power of God to dwell in him (2 Cor 12:7–10). The sufferings also helped him know Christ better; this manifested in a strong personal relationship with Christ and in the knowledge of the power of his resurrection (Phil 3:10). Identification with the death and resurrection of Jesus Christ helped Paul in his sanctification and prepared him for the final resurrection (Phil 3:11).

Third, the sufferings of Christ are the authentication of a true servant of Christ (Gal 6:17). Paul speaks to the Corinthians referring to himself, Apollos, and Cephas as servants of Christ and stewards of the gospel (1 Cor 4:1–5). Paul provides a set of criteria by which authentic servanthood can be measured (2 Cor 6:3–10; 11:23–33). As Howell rightly suggests:

> The first catalogue, a portrait of godly conduct in a context of trouble, establishes the credibility of his claim to be the true servant of God (2 Cor 3:4). The second catalogue is offered as a foolish boast (2 Cor 11:16–18, 21) to counteract the patently ridiculous claim of the "super apostles" (2 Cor 11:5; 12:11) to be the servants of Christ (2 Cor 11:23). If you want to recognize true servants, Paul says, observe the level of their sacrificial imitation of the suffering servant. Paul's résumé lists . . . only imprisonments (2 Cor 11:23), tortures (2 Cor 11:23–25), dangers (2 Cor 11:25–26), physical deprivations (2 Cor 11:27), internal pressures (2 Cor 11:28) and heart aches (2 Cor 11:29).[51]

---

50. J. D. G. Dunn, *The Theology of the Apostle Paul* (Grand Rapids: Eerdmans, 1998), 485, see also pages 482–87. There is an eschatological dualism that integrates the past, present, and future dimension of salvation. Dunn observes that when Paul speaks of the believer's identification with Christ's death and resurrection (Rom 6:5; Gal 2:19; 6:14), the present is conditioned in the light of the past and the future ("the already" and "the not yet"), that is by the transformed character and empowered living. See Howell, "Paul's Theology of Suffering," 99.

51. Howell, "Paul's Theology of Suffering," 100, 101.

Methodology

This book is based on the Pauline literature viewed from a disability perspective. The study is exegetical, analytical, and theological in nature with a reflection of disability in personal narrative form. I also share from personal experience to contextualise the discussion. What changes I have made in my perspectives of life as a mother of a child with special needs and what does my child teach me? The book also stems from my own experience of working with families having children with disabilities. I write as an advocate to give a ray of hope in the midst of uncertainties and painful experiences, and hope this book will be interesting to those directly and indirectly connect with disability. The hard realities of life sometimes lead the victims to question the meaning and purpose of the ongoing hardships for the disabled who are suffering, and of the non-disabled who are working and caring for them. The question sometimes arises: "Am I a burden to others?"

As human beings, we cannot always be good carers since there are times when we are tired, puzzled, confused, and pressured by others' attitudes and arrowed words. In the midst of these mixed approaches for those engaged in caring for someone with disability – the person with disability's own identity, a carer's/mother's identity, and society's expectations – how can a disabled person live a fulfilled life?

The Bible speaks about healing as the ultimate end of these hard realities. I was born and brought up in a Pentecostal context. I experienced and witnessed miraculous healing in the lives of people and heard sermons affirming that healing is impossible due to the unbelief of the person. There is truth in these experiences, and I have taught my students the significance of miracles in one's personal life and, being a minister, how to pray for others' healing. In the Gospel of Mark, Jesus could not do miracles because of people's unbelief (Mark 6:5–6). However, when it becomes my own experience, I am cautious in dealing with the scriptural texts.

In August 2013, when the doctor suggested that Jyothish needed surgery on his femur bone, it was hard to accept. For a week, I pondered on the issue in order to take a decision, and to ask God the reason for the delay in his healing. Meanwhile, in a class on the disability perspective, as I was teaching the students on the healing of the man born blind, my thought got anchored in Jesus's different ways of doing miracles. Jesus healed with a word, touch, exorcism, etc. However, in this passage, Jesus healed by applying mud on a man's eyes and asked him to walk to the pool of Siloam (John 9:6–7). Why did Jesus use this method for a blind person? Why did Jesus ask him to walk further? Was it because there was no water where he stood?

The whole chapter (John 9) is devoted to one miracle – the man born blind. The Pharisees come to Jesus with the question of stigma and taboos of Jewish society (John 9:34; compare 9:2). They are anxious to find the reason behind his disability, but the man is anxious to receive healing. The priority of the two groups is remarkable here in this narrative: the blind man with his parents and the Pharisees. The point that struck me in this passage was that Jesus had special purposes in dealing with people. The distance the blind man was asked to walk till the pool of Siloam can be seen as a delay in healing. Jesus used the incident to teach the hard-hearted Pharisees an eye-opening truth, namely, that their preference should be human rather than philosophical and ideological (e.g. healing on the Sabbath). Jesus talks about the reason for man's blindness as being to glorify the name of the Lord (John 9:3).

My interaction with families having children with disability and the teaching series with theological students on disability perspectives motivated me to write this book on the Pauline perspective on suffering – hence the phrase, "thorn in the flesh," is cautiously interpreted as disability since it is a debilitating issue related to disability.[52] Disability is a continuous condition and the person with disability is always under pressure. Persons with disabilities need source of strength and encouragement to move on in this journey.

Paul, who is called for a mission to complete God's purpose, receives strength and power from God himself. Instead of receiving healing, he receives the grace of God and the power to move on in his mission in the context of his continuing illness or disability. In this book, I analyse the passages in Paul's letters that help to identify the problems faced by the persons with disabilities and their families. The focus is mainly on the Corinthian letters where Paul speaks about weakness, foolishness, and divine power; and how the person without disability can accept the person with disability without stigmatization and prejudice, in order to affirm the place of the person with disability in the body of Christ.

---

52. Debilitating illness and disability are perhaps overlapping categories – they often go together, but don't always – but they are sufficiently similar to mean that how Paul speaks about his "thorn in the flesh" can be applied to the experience of a person with disability. See Royal L. Pakhuongte, *Paul's Suffering and Weakness in 2 Corinthians: Reading from a Disability Perspective* (Carlisle: Langham Academic, 2022), 209–11.

2

Disability in Antiquity
Judaism and Greco-Roman World

Introduction

In order to understand the Pauline perspective on disability, it is important to know the background of the Pauline epistles, namely, the Greco-Roman world. The terms "disabled" and "non-disabled" did not exist for Greeks or Romans. Some of the most common terms used are maimed (*pēros/mancus*), mutilated (*kolobos/curtus*), ugliness (*aischros/deformitas*), weakness (*astheneia/firmitas*), lameness in the leg (*chōlos/tardipes*), and club foot (*kullos*).[1]

Disability in Greco-Roman World

Deformity and disability were common in the ancient world due to malnutrition, disease, congenital problems, accidents, etc. There were also congenital and acquired deformities and disabilities. The concept of disability in Greco-Roman context is different from the modern notion because of the absence of the term "disabled" in the ancient context. The matters of enquiry are similar to the modern notion of disability, such as: the proportion of the disabled people in the ancient world falling into different categories like lame, blind, deaf, or other types of disabilities; the social status of the disabled; social stigma; the response to the defective births of children.

---

1. Nicole Kelley, "Deformity and Disability in Greece and Rome," in *This Abled Body: Rethinking Disabilities in Biblical Studies*, ed. Hector Avalos Sarah Melcher and Jeremy Schipper (Atlanta: SBL, 2007), 33.

The Disabled Greek God: Hephaestus

Hephaestus is described as a "solitary misfit among an un-ageing population of divine perfect deities" and "he is also the only major Olympian deity to have a physical handicap."² The different descriptions given to his condition were "ἀμφιγυήεις (both feet crooked); χωλός (lame); κυλλοποδίων (clubfooted; Hom *Il* 8.371, 20.270, 21.331); ἠπεδανος (weakly); as well as having ἀραιαι κνήμαι (slender legs) and being ῥικνος ποδας (withered of foot)."³

Congenital Deformity and Disability

Hephaestus's condition helps us to understand disability in the ancient world, especially congenital disability. He was born with a deformed foot although his limp was an acquired disability.⁴ Odyssey records his words to Zeus, "Aphrodite, daughter of Zeus, scorns me for that I am lame and loves destructive Ares because he is comely and strong of limb, whereas I was born misshapen. Yet for this is none other to blame but my two parents – would they have never begotten me."⁵ Hephaestus's mother, Hera states in the *Homeric Hymn to Pythian Apollo*, "But my son Hephaestus whom I bare was weakly among all the blessed gods and shrivelled of foot, a shame and a disgrace to me in heaven, whom I myself took in my hands and cast out so that he fell in the great sea."⁶

From the above statements, it is made clear that the lameness of Hephaestus is congenital. At this point, it is important to understand the attitude of Romans and Greeks towards congenital abnormality. The Romans and the Greeks responded differently to abnormal births. As Kelley notes:

> In the ancient world such birth functioned as a type of divination, although there is no evidence to suggest that ancient Greeks kept official records of these events or attempted to expiate them. Romans, by contrast, kept annual records of such events (writings

---

2. Robert Garland, *The Eye of the Beholder: Deformity and Disability in the Graeco-Roman World* (Ithaca: Cornell University Press), 61. See also Kelly, "Deformity and Disability," 35.

3. Kelley, "Deformity and Disability," 35. Kelly includes citations from Euterpe Bazapoulou-Kyrkanidou, "What Makes Hephaestus Lame?," *American Journal of Medical Genetics*, 72: 144–55, 146–49.

4. Garland, *Eye of the Beholder*, 62–63.

5. A. T. Murray (trans.), Homer, *The Odyssey*, 2 vols. (LCL, Cambridge: Harvard University, 1919), 8.308–312; see also Kelley, "Deformity and Disability," 36.

6. Hugh G. Evelyn White (trans.), *The Homeric Hymns and Homerica* (LCL, Cambridge: University, 1914). *Homeric Hymn to Pythian Apollo*, 316–18; See also Kelley, "Deformity and Disability," 36.

of Livy), which they regarded as a sign that the sacred *paxdeorum* or "covenant with the gods" had been broken.[7]

In Greek literature, there are four relevant passages – three pointing to an idealized picture and one to real-life situations.[8] Book five of Plato's *Republic* (406c) describes Plato's utopian state, in which the good offspring are to be cared for but "the offspring of the inferior, and any of those of the other sort who are born defective, they will properly dispose of in secret so that no one will know what has become of them."[9] This reference shows that the practice of exposure of the maimed was not normal in Plato's day as the term "in secret" refers to the concealment of the maimed or mutilated.[10] Aristotle's *Politics* also upholds the vision of the ideal state in relation to the bringing up of children with disabilities: "As to exposing or rearing the children born, let there be law that no deformed child (πεπηρωμενον) shall be reared."[11]

Plutarch throws light on the practice in ancient Sparta of

> examining infants to determine whether they might be worth rearing. The elders inspected each child: "infants who were 'sound and strong in the body' were ordered to be raised, while 'low-born and misshapen' infants were deposited at a place called the Apothetae, a chasm beneath Mount Taygetus."[12]

Plutarch's narrative (first or second century CE) may picture the state of the idealised past in Sparta, but it did not describe the then present condition. In other words, the source is reliable in the sense it presents the utopian vision of Plato and Aristotle.[13]

Soranus (a second century CE document) explicitly states a set of criteria for determining an infant's fitness.

---

7. Kelley, "Deformity and Disability," 36, n.4; Garland, *Eye of the Beholder*, 65, 67, emphasis added.

8. Martha L. Rose, *The Staff of Oedipus: Transforming Disability in Ancient Greece* (Ann Arbor: University of Michigan, 2003), 31–34.

9. Paul Shorey (trans.), *Plato, The Republic*, 2 vols. (LCL, Cambridge: Harvard University, 1953).

10. G. Van N. Viljoen, "Plato and Aristotle on the Exposure of Infants at Athens," *Acta Classica*, 1959, 2:58–69.

11. H. Rackham (trans.), *Aristotle, The Politics* (LCL, Cambridge: Harvard University Press, 1944).

12. Kelley, "Deformity and Disability," 37.

13. Rose, *The Staff of Oedipus*, 34.

A baby worth rearing should have a mother who experienced a healthy pregnancy, a suitable gestational age, and a vigorous cry. It should, moreover, be "perfect in all its parts, members and senses," with every body part properly moving and appropriately sized. "And by conditions contrary to those mentioned, the infant not worth rearing is recognized."[14]

The above evidence, except for Soranus's account, gives us an unclear picture of the type of deformity or disability suitable for exposure. Plato's and Aristotle's documents indicate that some Greeks decided to bring up congenitally abnormal infants.

It is interesting to wonder whether the mothers who gave birth to abnormal infants had the same attitude as Hera's disgust, revulsion, abandonment, or whether killing was a common norm in Greek society. Rose agrees that physical deformities may be seen as "blemishes" but she resists interpreting the ancient practice through modern assumptions. She suggests,

> In the ancient world, one would not have been shocked to deliver a baby with some anomaly or other. Childbirth was not a medical occasion, abnormal babies were not pathologized, and in fact the health and illness of infants and children were not of medical interest. A deformed baby was not necessarily seen as inferior, unattractive or in need of medical care: those assumptions are formed by modern medical and cultural values.[15]

However, Garland is of the view that most parents responded like Hera to their physically abnormal infant, namely, with revulsion that led to abandonment, exposure, or infanticide. We can assume (with caution) that the attitude of abandonment and revulsion cannot be taken to have been general, since babies with abnormalities would not have been necessarily rejected as "medically fragile and economically burdensome."[16]

The condition of the infants born abnormal in ancient Rome is obvious in two accounts: that of Dionysius of Halicarnassus and a code known as "Twelve Tables" (a fifth century BCE Roman law). The former reports that Romulus ordered all inhabitants of the city to bring up all their male descendants and not to kill (that is, allow to die) any child before the age of three, unless the child

---

14. Kelley, "Deformity and Disability," 37; Owsei Temkin (trans.), *Soranus' Gynaecology* (Baltimore: John Hopkins, 1956), 2.10; Rose, *The Staff of Oedipus*, 33.
15. Rose, *The Staff of Oedipus*, 36.
16. Kelley, "Deformity and Disability," 38.

was deformed or monstrous, in which case it was to be put to death immediately after birth. He did not stand in the way of such children being exposed on condition that the parents had shown them to five neighbours.[17] It is necessary to think of the existence of such law as pointing to an idealized past.[18]

The Twelve Tables code is referred to in a treatise by Cicero which makes the killing of deformed children a requirement. It is mentioned by Quintus regarding the legal power of the people's tribune. "[A]fter it had been quickly killed, as the twelve tables direct terribly deformed infants shall be killed, it was soon revived again, somehow or other, and as its second birth was even more hideous and abominable than before."[19] Garland suggests that there is no evidence for the prosecution of parents who brought up a deformed child. Moreover, we have evidence of the rearing of congenitally abnormal infants: examples include the emperor Claudius and the case of the congenitally mute Quintus Pedius.[20]

The Deformed and Disabled as Entertainment[21]

Many people in ancient Greece and Rome faced mockery and derision due to their physical deformity or disability. Claudius's mother referred to him as a monster and his sister Livilla hoped that Romans could avoid the cruel fate of having him as an emperor.[22] In his treatise *On Oratory*, Cicero states that "in deformity [*deformitatis*] and bodily disfigurement [*corporisvitiorum*] there is good material for making jokes."[23] In *Iliad*, there is a scene of the gods respond-

---

17. Dionysius of Halicarnassus, *Roman Antiquities, Volume II: Books 3–4*. Trans. Earnest Cary, LCL 347 (Cambridge: Harvard University, 1939), 2.15. Cited (slightly modified) by Kelley, "Deformity and Disability," 38, from W. den Boer, *Private Morality in Greece and Rome: Some Historical Aspects* (Leiden: Brill, 1979), 99. den Boer points to the familial rather than a civic responsibility to eliminate children with deformity and to exposure as an option rather than a requirement.

18. Garland, *Eye of the Beholder*, 16.

19. Marcus Tullius Cicero, *Laws*, trans. Francis Foster Barham (Edmund: Spettigue, 1942) 3.19; Cited by den Boer, 99; cf. Seneca the Elder, *Declamations, Volume II: Controversiae, Books 7–10. Suasoriae. Fragments*, trans. Michael Winterbottom, LCL 464 (Cambridge: Harvard University, 1974), 10.4.16.

20. Suetonius, *Claudius*, ed. J. Eugene Reed, Alexander Thomson (Philadelphia: Gebbie & Co., 1889), 3.2; Pliny, *Natural History*, trans. John Bostock and H. T. Riley (London: York, 1855), 35.21.

21. The terms "deformed" and "disabled" are used contextually.

22. Garland, *Eye of the Beholder*, 41. Suetonius, *Claudius* 3.2

23. Robert Garland, "The Mockery of the Deformed and Disabled in Graeco-Roman Culture," in *Laughter Down the Centuries*, vol 1, eds. Siegfried Jakel and Asko Timonen (Turku: TurunYliopsto, 1994), 75.

ing with laughter to the action of Hephaestus when he attempted to defuse the tension between Zeus and Hera (by playing the part of a wine steward at an Olympian feast): "But among the blessed immortals uncontrollable laughter went up as they saw Hephaestus bustling about the palace."[24] Here is a picture of others mocking Hephaestus.

Drinking feasts in both Greece and Rome appear often to have been events that included mockery of deformed and disabled people. Greek vase paintings depict "hunchbacks, cripples, dwarfs, and obese women" performing as entertainers, and Horace relates a story about two deformed men trading insults at a *convivium* for the entertainment of onlookers.[25] Lampridius reports that the emperor Elagabalus used to invite for dinner "eight bald men or eight one-eyed men or eight gout sufferers or eight deaf men . . . in order to arouse laughter."[26]

Another example given by Homer in the *Iliad* is that of Thersites, who is described in harsh and disapproving words. "This was the ugliest man who came beneath Ilion. He was bandy-legged and went lame of one foot, with shoulders stooped and drawn together over his chest, and above this his skull went up to a point with the wool grown sparsely upon it."[27] This gives an idea of the physiognomy of the ancient world, which made the entire army burst into laughter at Thersites.

Deformed individuals were also seen as a form of personal entertainment in the late republican and early imperial Rome. "The dwarf and the giant, the hunchback and the living skeleton ceased being prodigies and became pets; they ceased being destroyed and expiated and became objects of the attention and cultivation of every class."[28] Pliny records that Augustus's granddaughter Julia retained a dwarf named Cinopas as a pet. Plutarch mentions the existence of a "monster market" in Rome.[29] Moreover, there was a great demand

---

24. Richmond Lattimore (trans.), *The Iliad of Homer* (Chicago: University of Chicago, 1951), 1.599–600.

25. Garland, *Eye of the Beholder*, 84–85. Horace, *Satire* 1.5, 50–70. See also Garland, "Mockery of the Deformed," 73.

26. Cited by Garland, *Eye of the Beholder*, 85–86. *Heliogabalus* 29.3. See also Kelley, "Deformity and Disability," 40.

27. Trans. Lattimore, *The Iliad of Homer*, 2:217–19; 2:225–42; 2:270.

28. Carlin A. Barton, *The Sorrows of the Ancient Romans: The Gladiator and the Monster* (Princeton: Princeton University, 1993), 86.

29. Pliny, *Natural History*, 7:74–75. Plutarch, *Moralia*, Harold North Fowler (trans.), 14 vols. LCL (Cambridge: Harvard University, 1927), 520c.

of *distorti*, which caused children to be made intentionally deformed for the purpose of increasing market value.[30]

Economic and Career Prospects of the Disabled

In ancient Greece and Rome, there is evidence to show that the deformed and disabled were not necessarily economically weak or dependent on family and friends for their livelihood. Hephaestus's works were much valued although he was mocked by his friends at dinners and described as "a cunning black-smith whose professional skills are highly admired and secretly feared, and whose social skills should not be underrated."[31] Physically handicapped people were involved in a wide range of economic activities.[32] Some artisans are reported to have some form of physical impairment, for example, a tailor who has a limp and a lame peddler. People with deformities could also be singers, dancers, and the like.[33] They even served in the military.[34] Blind people appear as mythological and historical figures, as poets, musicians, and prophets.[35] The political status of the disabled cannot be understood clearly, and the economic status reveals that they possibly had an independent status.

Blindness in Ancient Greece and Rome

Blindness is the most common physical handicap in the ancient texts; it was widespread in the ancient world. The causes of blindness were seen as being primarily due to natural causes and as punishment from the gods. Moreover, people were blinded in antiquity due to accidental damage to the eyes in the

---

30. Barton, *The Sorrows of the Ancient Romans*, 86. W. H. Fyfe (trans.), Longinus, *De sublimitate* (1927) 44:5. See also Kelley, "Deformity and Disability," 40.

31. Simon Hornblower and Anthony Spawforth, eds. *The Oxford Classical Dictionary* 3rd ed. (Oxford and New York: Oxford University, 1996), 82. Homer, *Odyssey* 7.91–93; 4.617; Homer, *Hymn* 20.1; *Iliad* 1.571; 18.143; *Odyssey* 8.286 give evidence of his art and skilled work. See also Kelley, "Deformity and Disability," 39, 41.

32. Rose, *The Staff of Oedipus*, 40.

33. Alciphron, *Letters of Farmers,* 24:1; Aristophanes, "Anagyrus" frag. 57 PCG; Garland, *Eye of the Beholder*, 32–33.

34. Homer, *Iliad* 2:216–19; Plutarch, *Moralia*, Harold North Fowler (trans.), 14 vols. LCL (Cambridge: Harvard University, 1927), 234e, 241e, 331b; Demosthenes, *On the Crown*, 67; Rose, *The Staff of Oedipus*, 40.

35. DioChrysostum, *Oratory* 36:10–11; Homer, *Odyssey* 8:62–70; Pausanius 7:5. It is impossible to make a generalized conclusion; however, evidence reveals that a few engaged in these occupations. Garland, *Eye of the Beholder*, 34. These occupations were made available to others also, and not only to persons with limited sight or blindness. Rose, *The Staff of Oedipus*, 91.

battle, contagious disease, vitamin A deficiency, old age, etc. Herodotus states that Cnidians received eye injuries as they broke stones while digging a trench[36] and Julius Caesar's account of the civil war mentions that four centurions in a single cohort were blinded in one battle.[37] The "Hippocratic authors and Galen recorded observations about cataracts, and Aristotle noted that blind parents sometimes gave birth to blind babies."[38]

Disability as Punishment

It was believed that Teiresias, a blind Theban prophet, was blinded as a punishment from the gods. The two different reasons for his blindness are widely known. In one version, Callimachus's fifth hymn, Teiresias is blinded because he saw Athena bathing; he was gifted with the talent of prophecy as his mother Chariclo intercedes on his behalf. In another version of the myth attributed to Hesiod and reported by Apollodorus, Teiresias is blinded by Hera: "There was a Theban seer called Teiresias. Herod says that he witnessed two snakes copulating on Mount Kyllene and when he wounded them, he became a woman from a man, but when he observed the same snakes copulating again, he turned into a man. For this Hera blinded him but Zeus granted him the gift of prophecy."[39] Here again we deal with gods and goddesses; however, little is known about the real experiences of the ancient Greeks and Romans.

Other mythological accounts are: Philip of Macedon lost an eye after seeing his wife with the god Ammon; Aipytos was blinded and died after entering the temple of Poseidon Hippios at Mantineia; Lycurgus was blinded by Zeus because of his persecution of Dionysus; Thamyris was blinded or maimed because he tried to compete with the Muses; Stesichorus regained his eyesight after making amends to Helen. In Greek myths, blindness was often given as a punishment for offences of mortals against other mortals.[40]

---

36. Herodotus 1:174; Rose, *The Staff of Oedipus*, 82.

37. Julius Ceasar, *On the Civil War* (trans. W. A. McDevitte and W. S. Bohn, 1994), 3:53; Garland, *Eye of the Beholder*, 85.

38. Kelley, "Deformity and Disability," 42. Hippocratic authors *On Vision* 9:4–5; Galen 10:990; Aristotle, *History of Animals* 585b.

39. Cited by Garland, *Eye of the Beholder*, 100–101; See also Kelley, "Deformity and Disability," 42. Apollodorus 3:6:7.

40. R. G. A. Buxton, "Blindness and Limits: Sophocles and the Logic of Myth," *The Journal of Hellenic Studies* 100, 1980: 22–37, 32; Plutarch, *Alexander* 3; Pausanius, 8:5:4–5; 10:3; Homer, *Iliad* 6:138–40; Plato, *Phaedrus* 243.

These examples show that blindness was generally seen as a punishment, although not necessarily in all cases. Furthermore, extraordinary abilities were also given to the blind in order to compensate the loss of eyesight.

Special Abilities of the Disabled

It is believed that in ancient Greece "loss of sight was linked by a kind of compensation magic to clairvoyance and the gift of poetic creation, song, and enchantment."[41] Examples of this include Teiresias who was compensated by talents such as the gift of poetry or prophecy such that, though blind, he was also known for his insight – which was often compared to that of Apollo.[42] Thamyris was both maimed and known for his musical talents and artisanal skills.[43] Herodotus mentions Evenius, who was blinded as punishment but compensated with the gift of prophecy. Pausanias reports that a blind fisherman named Phormion possessed the ability to have prophetic dreams, and Apollodorus mentions Phineus, who was blind but could foretell the future.[44] That blindness was also accompanied with the gift of other sensory perception is also agreed by ancient writers. "The blind remembers better, being released from having their faculty of memory engaged with objects of sight."[45]

I agree with Rose who affirms that, although blindness in mythology seems to be followed by compensatory gifts, we should doubt that was the case with all people who were blind (it is possible that blindness was a common condition in ancient Greece and Rome).[46] However, we can generally agree that blindness as punishment was believed to be accompanied by a talent or gift, but that belief varies in regard to time, place, and people. From the above examples, it seems that there were opportunities for people with disability to have advantageous career options and opportunities while, at times, also being treated as entertainment for others in the ancient world. On the other hand, the idea of disability as punishment and a matter of mockery was also prevalent.

---

41. Mirko D. Grmek, *Diseases in the Ancient Greek World*, trans. Mireille Muellner and Leonard Muellner (Baltimore: John Hopkins University, 1989), 25.

42. Aristotle, *Eudemian Ethics* 1248b; Sophocles, *Oedipus Tyrannus* 284–5; cf. Homer, *Odyssey*, 10:492–93.

43. Homer, *Iliad* 2:594–600.

44. Herodotus 9:93–94; Pausanias 7:5:7; Apollodorus 1:9:21.

45. Buxton, "Blindness and Limits," 29.

46. Rose, *The Staff of Oedipus*, 87.

Disability in Judaism

This section deals with the disability in Judaism with particular regard to priests in the temple.

The Priest's Perfection in the Temple

Regarding the priest's perfection in the temple, the Torah states that this mediator between heaven and earth should be without blemish, of pure lineage, and also ritually pure.[47]

> The LORD spoke to Moses, saying: Speak to Aaron and say: No one of your offspring throughout their generations who has a blemish may approach to offer the food of his God. For no one who has a blemish shall draw near, one who is blind or lame, or one who has a mutilated face or a limb too long, or one who has a broken foot or a broken hand, or a hunchback, or a dwarf, or a man with a blemish in his eyes or an itching disease or scabs or crushed testicles. No descendant of Aaron the priest who has a blemish shall come near to offer the LORD's offerings by fire; since he has a blemish, he shall not come near to offer the food of his God. He may eat the food of his God, of the most holy as well as of the holy. But he shall not come near the curtain or approach the altar, because he has a blemish, that he may not profane my sanctuaries; for I am the LORD; I sanctify them. Thus Moses spoke to Aaron and to his sons and to all the people of Israel. (Lev 21:16–24)

Although, a person with disabilities was not permitted to offer sacrifices, he was allowed to eat the sacrificial meal, which is part of a priest's function. Those excluded from the list are not readily visible defects such as deafness, mental illness, and mental disability. But in the rabbinic system, these features are included and are significant.[48] In the most perfect place, namely, the temple, the people without blemish are allowed to offer sacrifices.

The taxonomy of animals offered as sacrifice is also linked to the list of eleven blemishes that priests could possess.

---

47. Judith Z. Abrams, *Judaism and Disability: Portrayals in Ancient Texts from the Tanach through the Balvi* (Washington, DC: Gallaudet University, 1998), 23.

48. Sifra, *Emor* 3b:1 p.114. Tannaitic Midrash on Leviticus. For more information see Abrams, *Judaism and Disability*, 28.

> When anyone offers a sacrifice of well-being to the Lord, in fulfillment of a vow or as a freewill offering, from the herd or from the flock, to be acceptable it must be perfect; there shall be no blemish in it. Anything blind, or injured, or maimed, or having a discharge or an itch or scabs – these you shall not offer to the Lord or put any of them on the altar as offerings by fire to the Lord. An ox or a lamb that has a limb too long or too short you may present for a freewill offering; but it will not be accepted for a vow. Any animal that has its testicles bruised or crushed or torn or cut, you shall not offer to the Lord; such you shall not do within your land. (Lev 22:21–24)

Lev 21:1–22:16 speaks about the ritual purity of the priests, the family of the priests, the ritual purity of the high priests, marriage of high priests, and sacrificial offerings that a priest and priestly family must eat. Thus, this whole section of the Torah deals with priestly status and its maintenance through ritual purity, preservation of the lineage, etc. Moreover, it reveals that priests with disabilities were still priests, but they were excluded from officiating the cult. Abrams suggests, "Thus a priest in a state of ritual impurity is more disabled than a priest who is blind: while a blind priest may still consume the food set aside for him, a priest who is ritually impure cannot."[49]

In connection to this, the Mishnah details the Torah's descriptions of blemishes that disqualify priests from officiating the cult:

> There are more [disqualifications] for a person [than these, namely], a wedge-shaped head or a turnip-shaped head or a mallet-shaped head or a sunken head or [the head] flat behind, or a hunchback. Rabbi Yehudah declares [the humpbacked priest] qualified, but the sages disqualify [him].[50]

To the list of blemishes in Lev 21:16–24 that disqualify a priest, Sifra adds (in the Tannaitic Midrash on Leviticus) several visible blemishes and three "non-invisible" ones, namely, people with speaking and hearing disabilities, people with mental disabilities, and people who are intoxicated.

> I have nothing [here in Leviticus 21:16–24] but these [blemishes] alone. From whence [do we know] to augment [and include] other blemishes? Scripture says, "blemish" (21:17) [and it says in the

---

49. Abrams, *Judaism and Disability*, 26.
50. M. Bekorot 7:1; Abrams, *Judaism and Disability*, 28.

> next verse] "blemish" (21:18). From whence [do we know that] the negro and the lame [person] and the one with white spots on his face and the hunchback and the dwarf and the deaf-mute and the mentally ill and the drunkard and [those with] ritually pure plagues [cannot officiate in the cult]? Scripture says, "a man" (21:17) [and] "a man" (21:18) to augment [the meaning].[51]

An intoxicated person, who was disqualified from the cultic service due to his uncontrolled behaviour, is similar to those with speaking disabilities and mental disabilities.

B. Meggillah describes the story of Rav Sheshet who was blind, stating that his disability protects him from God's lethal presence, from which most sages must flee, in a synagogue made of stones after the First Temple ruins.

> Rav Sheshet was [once] sitting in the synagogue which "moved and settled" in Nehardea, when the *Shekhinah* [God's presence] came. He did not go out [of the synagogue as did other sages when the Shekhinah approached]. The ministering angels came and [tried to] scare him [away]. He Rav Sheshet said to Him [God]: "Master of the Universe, if one is afflicted and one is not afflicted, who gives way to whom?" God [then] said to them [the angels]: "Leave him."[52]

Rav Sheshet, who was unable to flee from God's presence, asked for mercy and was granted with it. He had great insight and was enlightened in his disabling condition of blindness while sighted human beings must flee from it – leading to blinded insight.[53]

Body Metaphor

The human body is used as a metaphor for society, its values, and beliefs and is sometimes linked with the divine. Mary Douglas argues that:

> The body is a model which can stand for any bounded system. Its boundaries can represent any boundaries that are threatened

---

51. Sifra *Emor* 3b:1, p.114; Abrams, *Judaism and Disability*, 28.

52. B. Meggillah 29a; Rav Sheshet (290–320). According to the tradition, the Jewish community in Nehardea was ancient and was first settled in the sixth century BCE. The synagogue built there by the exiles in 586 BCE brought from the site of the Temple, where the Shekkeinah moved and settled. Abrams, *Judaism and Disability*, 208.

53. Abrams, *Judaism and Disability*, 30.

and precarious. The body is a complex structure. The functions of its different parts and their relation afford a source of symbols for other complex structures . . . [We must be] prepared to see in the body a society, and to see the powers and dangers credited to social structure reproduced in small on the human body.[54]

In 1 Corinthians, Paul compared the church to the body of Christ and the members of the church to different organs of the body, showing the unity of the body and the different functions of the organs in the body.

If each person is a working organ and part of the body, that is society, how should people with disabilities be incorporated to this metaphor? The metaphors for disabilities vary according to culture and language for disabilities are valued and constructed differently in different cultures; for example, in the Bavli, "All human bodies are carriers; happy are they who are worthy of being respectable of the Torah."[55]

Conclusion

The preceding discussions on disability in the Greco–Roman world and Judaism have given us a glimpse of the perspectives in antiquity towards the people with disability. Hephaestus's condition of congenital disability illustrates the ideal attitude towards people with disability and their parents in antiquity, although, in reality, society members responded differently. Some related the birth of the disabled child to some type of divination, while others had a completely negative view of it as punishment from gods. Parents often responded to their abnormal infant with revulsion that led to abandonment, exposure, and infanticide. Moreover, many disabled people faced mockery and derision due to their physical deformity and disability. The economic and career prospects of people with disability also varied in antiquity as there is evidence some had an independent status. Finally, Judaism speaks about the priest's perfection in the temple – which required individuals who were without blemish, pure of lineage, and ritually pure.

---

54. Mary Douglas, *Purity and Danger: An Analysis of Concepts of Pollution and Taboo* (New York: Praeger, 1966), 117. In India, society is envisaged as a body, with the different castes as organs of that body. See George Lakoff, *Women, Fire and Dangerous Things: What Categories Reveal about Mind* (Chicago: University of Chicago, 1987), 274.

55. Talmud Bavli, 74; B. Sanhedrin 99b.

3

The Identity of the Weak in 1 Corinthians

Introduction

The immediate context of Paul's address to the Corinthians involves internal factions and problems in the church, alluded to in 1 Corinthians 1:10–12. However, the epistle points to Paul's emphasis on the community and unity within it – focusing on each one walking in their new identity received through the divine grace manifested in the cross of Christ. As Thiselton comments, "*whether the issue of discord is dominant or merely a constituent component of a wide set of problems,* not *ecclesiology* but *a re-proclamation of grace and the cross to Christian believers takes centre stage.*"[1] It is the building up of the community through the example of Christ, his grace and cross, and working in mutuality and love, that helps one embrace differences and weaknesses. This is materialised in the respect and honour shown towards "the other" and has a very significant impact in our relationships to the less honourable, the weak, and the vulnerable.

This chapter primarily considers God's reversal of cultural norms in choosing the foolish and what this means for persons with disabilities, drawing upon 1 Corinthians 1:18–2:7. The following chapter considers: the spiritual gifts and talents of the person with disability (drawing primarily from 1 Cor 12:4–11); the place of the person with disability in the body of Christ (based upon 1 Cor 12:12–31); love that embraces weakness (in an analysis of 1 Cor 13); and the place of the person with disability in the resurrection (based on 1 Cor 15:35–58).

---

1. A. C. Thiselton, *The First Epistle to the Corinthians: A Commentary on the Greek Text* (Grand Rapids: Eerdmans, 2000), 34. (Italics original.)

God Chooses the Foolish (1 Cor 1:18–2:7)

It seems quite paradoxical that Paul speaks about God choosing the foolish in a context where honour and status were given much importance. Furthermore, he speaks to the Corinthians about the reversal of status, strong and weak, wise and foolish. The paradox of God's wisdom and the wisdom of the world was dealt with in the cross of Christ. Hence, Paul speaks about the power in the proclamation of the cross of Christ (1:18–25), the status of the Corinthians (1:26–31), and Paul's weakness when he first came to Corinth (2:1–5).

The Cross as the Foundation in Wisdom and Folly (1:18–25)

The contrast in 1 Corinthians 1:18 regarding a person being in the way of ruin and one in the way of salvation corresponds to the contrast between human folly (*mōria*) and the power of God, rather than the contrast between human folly and human wisdom.[2] The wisdom–folly contrast played an important role in the Greco-Roman world and it appeared in the slogans and catch words at Corinth.[3] As Thiselton suggests, "*Paul transposes the wisdom–folly contrast into that between what is humanly self-defeating, stultifying, and foolish on one side and what becomes effective, operative, powerful, and transformative* by divine agency."[4] The proclamation of the cross is the criterion for this contrast; in other words, God and the proclamation of the cross are in contrast to the wisdom of the world. "The proclamation is *folly* unless God, not human wisdom, stands behind it to validate or underwrite it."[5]

The proclamation of the cross is the power of God and there are different nuances for power in the New Testament. Power means authority, force, influ-

---

2. H. Conzelmann, *1 Corinthians: A Commentary*, Hermeneia (Eng. trans., Philadelphia: Fortress, 1975), 41.

3. "Folly" (*mōria*) occurs in the New Testament in 1 Corinthians (1:18, 21, 23; 2:14; and 3:19); while "fool" or "foolish" (*mōroō*) occurs in the Pauline epistles in 1 Corinthians (1 Cor 1:25, 27; 3:18; and 4:10; cf. 2 Tim 2:13; Tit 3:9).

4. Thiselton, *First Epistle to the Corinthians*, 154 (italics original). See also A. C. Thiselton, "The Meaning of σάρξ in 1 Cor 5:5: A Fresh Approach in the Light of Logical and Semantic Factors," *STJ* 26 (1973): 204–28. Paul uses this rhetorical technique of transposition or code switching elsewhere.

5. Thiselton, *First Epistle to the Corinthians*, 155. (Emphasis original.) Barth suggests, "The promise of the Word of God is not an empty pledge . . . it is the transposing of man into the wholly new state of one who has accepted and appropriated the promise." Barth, CD, 1/1, *The Doctrine of the Word of God*, sect. 3.120.

ence, etc.⁶ It refers to the power of the Holy Spirit (Acts 1:8); deeds manifesting great power (Luke 1:51; Acts 2:22); "authorities and power" (Col 1:16; Eph 2:12); and competency (Acts 18:24). It is significant that "δυναμόω may mean to empower someone in the sense of giving them competence or authorisation, while δύναμαι means to have the ability to carry something through or able to do it."⁷ The cross constitutes the central theme of this passage as it is the means through which God's power is active and thus also his presence and promise about transformation and accomplishment. This is different from human wisdom and folly in its quality and kind.

Paul is aware of the Corinthians' practice of associating wisdom with degrees of human achievement, which is opposite to the proclamation of the cross, where the cross is a sign of humiliation, curse, dishonour, and even disability. In Greek philosophical schools, some perceived hardships as a sign of authenticity, whereas in the case of some rhetorical schools, only applause is perceived as a sign of success.⁸

Paul's theology has its foundation on the proclamation of the cross, where the pattern of Christian discipleship is living for others – no matter the cost. Bonhoeffer writes, "If it is I who say where God will be, I will always find there a [false] God who . . . corresponds to me, is agreeable to me . . . But if it is God who says where he will be . . . that place is the cross of Christ."⁹

In Paul's letters power appears as weakness and weakness as power. Thus, he may be condemning the Corinthians' approach to power without the cross and their thirst for human riches and power (1 Cor 4:8). Instead, he offers them a cruciform lifestyle: "Paul adopts a cruciform posture in relation to 'power.'"¹⁰ This idea is further developed by Moltmann, who suggests that "Christian identity can be understood as an act of identification with the crucified Christ."¹¹

---

6. Grundmann, δύναμαι, *TDNT* ed. Gerhard Kittel, trans. & ed. Geoffrey W. Bromiley, Vol II (Grand Rapids: Eerdmans, 1964), 284–317 at 286; W. Bauer, W. F. Arndt, F. W. Gingrich and F. W. Danker, *Greek-English Lexicon of the New Testament, and Other Early Christian Literature*, 3rd edition (London: University of Chicago, 2000), 207.

7. Thiselton, *First Epistle to the Corinthians*, 155–56.

8. John T. Fitzgerald, *Cracks in an Earthen Vessel–An Examination of the Catalogues of Hardships in the Corinthian Correspondence* SBLDS 99 (Atlanta: Scholars, 1988), 117–50 and 203–7; Stanley K. Stowers, "Paul on the Use and Abuse of Reason," in *Greeks, Romans and Christians: Essays in Honour of J. Malherbe*, eds. D. L. Balch, E. Ferguson, and Wayne Meeks (Minneapolis: Augsburg, 1990), 253–86.

9. D. Bonhoeffer, *Meditating on the Word* (Eng. trans., Cambridge: Cowley, 1986), 45. See also D. Bonhoeffer, *The Cost of Discipleship* (Eng. trans. London: SCM, abridged. 1959), 35–36.

10. Thiselton, *First Epistle to the Corinthians*, 157.

11. J. Moltmann, *The Crucified God*, trans. R. A. Wilson and John Bowden (London: SCM, 1975), 19.

This means a state of humiliation rather than power by sharing in the "abuse of Christ" (Heb 11:26) and living in solidarity with the humiliated and vulnerable, where those at Corinth were often called "weak."[12] Paul quotes the Old Testament in verse twenty: "has not God made a fool of the world's wisdom." Chrysostom suggests that "the event of the cross is like a new frame of reference brought to the sick by health, or to children or to the unsound in mind by full, rational maturity."[13]

Paul contrasted the way in which the world came to know God, not through wisdom but through the foolishness of what is proclaimed (1 Cor 1:21). Here Paul seems to be referring to the content of the preaching rather than the proclamation of the crucified Christ.[14] Verses twenty-two to twenty-five further support the contention that Paul is referring here to the content of the preaching, namely, "the foolishness of what was preached." Thiselton agrees that the wisdom of God can be understood as:

1. Wisdom revealed in the law and the prophets
2. A transformative system which reverses the value system of the world
3. Divine wisdom as God's self-disclosure
4. Divine wisdom as prophetic critique of instrumental reason
5. The wisdom of God as grace freely given.[15]

The wisdom of the world is opposite to the wisdom of God; the wisdom of the Corinthians "embodies the self-sufficient, self-confident *stance* which is at variance with the 'weakness' and self-emptying of the cross and of the cruciform nature of God's dealing with the world in Christ."[16]

In Jewish–Hellenistic and the Greco–Roman worlds, wisdom is seen as success, achievement, and a way to honour and status; the cross of Christ is seen

---

12. J. Moltmann, *The Way of Jesus Christ* (Minneapolis: Fortress, 1995), 210; and *Theology of Hope* (Eng. trans. London: SCM, 1967), 304–38.

13. J. Chrysostom, *Homilies on the Epistle of Paul to the Corinthians* English NPNF. Ed, P. Schaff (Edinburgh: T&T Clark, 1887–94; Grand Rapids: Eerdmans, 1989), 4.1–4; Thiselton, *First Epistle to the Corinthians*, 166.

14. Most scholars agree with the content of the preaching: H. A. W. Meyer, *Critical and Exegetical Handbook to the Epistle to the Corinthians* (Eng. trans., 2 vols. Edinburgh: T&T Clark, 1892), 1:42; C. Wolff, *Der erste Brief des Paulus an die Korinther* (*Paul's First Letter to the Corinthians*), THKNT 7 (Leipzig: EvangelischeVerlagsanstalt, 1996), 39; R. A. Horsley, *1 Corinthians* (Nashville: Abingdon, 1998), 51. Kerygma is not the act of preaching but the content of preaching.

15. Thiselton, *First Epistle to the Corinthians*, 168, 169.

16. Thiselton, *First Epistle to the Corinthians*, 169.

as the opposite of these. For Jews and Greeks as they seek signs and wisdom, the cross of Christ is a stumbling block on their way to success. But for those who are called, the cross of Christ is God's power and God's wisdom. God's wisdom cannot be understood in human terms as signs or techniques; it is manifested in a different way, in other words, "the way of love which accepts the constraints imposed by the human condition or plight and the prior divine act of promise, and becomes effective and operative (has **power**) in *God's own way*, for it corresponds with God's own nature as revealed in Christ and in the cross."[17] Jungel writes, "God defined himself as love on the cross of Christ."[18]

God's wisdom is revealed in Christ as Christ himself and his cross subvert worldly assumptions and standards. It is the power active in weakness (1 Cor 1:18) and is reflected in the hardships of the apostle (the cruciform lifestyle) (4:9–13). God was pleased to call a few and for those who were called (1 Cor 1:21), divine wisdom stands in contrast to the achievements of human wisdom. The discussion on God's wisdom is brought to a conclusion in verse 25, "God's foolishness is wiser than human wisdom and God's weakness is stronger than human strength." Margaret Mitchell comments,

> The gospel story, as the exemplification of God's paradoxical logic, necessarily entails a re-evaluation of σοφία, δύναμις, and, εὐγενής ("wisdom, power and noble birth") which dismantles the "human" constructs which are still so operative in the Corinthians' lives and dealings with one another. In place of all this, the gospel offers Christ crucified, a new kind of *sōphia* ("wisdom") as 1 Corinthians 1:30 recapitulates.[19]

When Paul speaks of the power of the cross in weakness, the contrast between worldly values and Paul's idea of power is striking. That God's foolishness is wiser than humans means that this cannot be understood with limited human wisdom and power. "The role of the cross as foundation and criterion

---

17. Thiselton, *First Epistle to the Corinthians*, 172. Bold and italics original.

18. E. Jungel, *God as the Mystery of the World: On the Foundation of the Theology of the Crucified One in the Dispute between Theism and Atheism* (London: Bloomsbury, 2014), 220; *Theological Essays* (Eng. trans. Edinburgh: T&T Clark, 1989), 1:65. Jungel identifies the cross as the world's turning point and "is the foundation and measure of metaphorical language about God, then such language itself has the function of bringing about a turning around, or change of direction. God cannot be spoken of as if everything remained as it was."

19. M. M. Mitchell, "Rhetorical Shorthand in Pauline Argumentation: The Function of 'the Gospel' in the Corinthian Correspondence," in *Gospel in Paul: Studies on Corinthians, Galatians and Romans* for R. N. Longenecker, ed. by L. A. Jervis and P. Richardson, JSNT Supplement Series 108 (Sheffield: Sheffield Academic, 1994), 65.

of authentic wisdom has been demonstrated from the conflict between the very nature of the cross and human aspirations and evaluations concerning wisdom and folly."[20]

The Reversal of Status (1 Cor 1:26–31)

The human evaluation of status, achievements, and success is reversed in the act of Jesus Christ on the cross and this becomes evident in how the Corinthian community is constituted (1:26–31). The majority of the members are not clever (*sophoi*), influential (*dunatoi*), or from a high social class (*eugeneis*). In the context of the Greco-Roman society, the Corinthians did not receive honour and Paul here speaks about a standard of measuring honour as "in the Lord" (1:31): "Let the one who claims honour establish that claim in the Lord."[21] The Corinthians have no chance to boast on their intellectual, political, and social achievements or in the honourable status of the city, but they have to value their achievements and success exclusively in light of Christ and in light of the "act of reversal brought about by God through Christ."[22]

God's calling emphasises the nature of the calling and God as the sole agent of the calling.[23] The calling refers to the conditions, circumstances, and also the manner of the calling – they are all sharing in the same grace, same circumstance, and same destiny as the term "brethren" denotes. Thiselton suggests, "In this passage, therefore, Paul compares the Corinthians' achievements in the realm of wisdom, influence, and status as humankind evaluates these on grounds of *esteem, glory, or honour*, and the corresponding status with God has accorded them through Christ in his own eyes."[24] There was a consensus among the scholars that the vast majority of the Christians at Corinth were of low social status[25] but some disagree on the basis that there were a few

---

20. Thiselton, *First Epistle to the Corinthians*, 176.

21. D. A. deSilva, "Let the One who Claims Honor Establish that Claim in the Lord: Honor Discourse in the Corinthian Correspondence," *BTB* 28 (1998): 61–74.

22. Thiselton, *First Epistle to the Corinthians*, 179.

23. R. F. Collins, *1 Corinthians*, Sacra Pagina 7 (Collegeville: Liturgical, 1999), 109. "According to the flesh" is understood as according to human standards.

24. Thiselton, *First Epistle to the Corinthians*, 180, 181. (Italics original.)

25. For more details on the consensus of the scholars, see D. G. Horrell, *The Social Ethos of the Corinthian Correspondence* (Edinburgh: T&T Clark, 1996), 91–101; also, G. Theissen, *The Social Setting of Pauline Christianity: Essays on Corinth*, trans. by J. H. Schulz (Philadelphia: Fortress, 1982), 69–120. Origen quotes Celsus, "Let no one educated, no one wise, no one sensible draw near" (Origen, *Against Celsus*, 3:44); Calvin comments that "the Corinthians . . . had no great standing in the world" (J. Calvin, *The First Epistle of Paul the Apostle to the Corinthians*,

distinguished people in the list of the called.²⁶ Theissen emphasises the social diversity of the first urban churches since the Corinthian church was marked by internal stratification²⁷ due to the presence of office holders (Crispus and Erastus); heads of households (Crispus and Stephanus); those who have wealth and affluence (Epaphroditus, Gaius, and Titus Justus); or those people who travel for business purposes (Phoebe, Aquila and Priscilla, Erastus, Stephanus, and Chloe's people). Witherington suggests

> The social level of the Corinthian Christians apparently varied from quite poor to rather well-off . . . a fair cross-section of city . . . Many . . . gained status not by lineage or sophistication . . . Paul's words in 1 Cor 1:26 would have been a pointed reminder to such status-hungry people of their origins.²⁸

Salvation in Christ cannot be measured according to human values, and it is the grace through the cross of Christ that makes them valuable among the entire society. As Witherington notes, "Salvation in Christ is not a human . . . self-improvement scheme, but a radical rescue . . . Grace is not only the great unifier but also the great leveller."²⁹ The terms, wise (*sophoi*), powerful (*dunatoi*) and of noble birth (*eugeneiō*) referto the sophists, whose parents are powerful and of noble birth, who have generations of wealth, fame, honour, influence, and also social and political power and have self-promotion in "boast and glory."³⁰ The transformative effect of the cross determines the Christian status; a gift of grace and God's free choice and has nothing to do with the self-promotion or self-glorification for being wise, powerful, and influential.

Calvin's New Testament Commentaries 9, trans. by J. W. Fraser, ed. by D. W. Torrance and T. F. Torrance [Grand Rapids: Eerdmans, 1960], 44). See also G. A. Deissmann, *Light from the Ancient Near East* (London: Hodder & Stoughton, 2nd ed., 1927), 144; E. A. Judge, *The Social Pattern of the Christian Groups in the First Century* (London: Tyndale, 1960), 60.

26. J. Moffatt, *The First Epistle of Paul to the Corinthians*, Moffatt New Testament Commentary 7 (London: Hodder & Stoughton, 1938), 19–20.

27. G. Thiessen, "Social Stratification in the Corinthian Community: A Contribution to the Sociology of Early Hellenistic Christianity," in *The Social Setting of Pauline Christianity: Essays on Corinth* (Eng. trans. Philadelphia: Fortress, 1982), 69–120, at 69.

28. B. Witherington, III, *Conflict and Community in Corinth: A Socio Rhetorical Commentary on 1 and 2 Corinthians* (Grand Rapids: Eerdmans, 1995), 23–24.

29. Witherington, *Conflict and Community*, 118.

30. B. W. Winter, *Philo and Paul among the Sophists*, Society for New Testament Studies Monograph Series 96 (Cambridge: Cambridge University, 1997), 189; Plutarch, *Moralia*, Harold North Fowler, trans. 14 vols. LCL (Cambridge: Harvard University, 1927), 58C; Diogenes Laertius, *Orations*, 29–32; E. L. Bowie, "The Importance of the Sophists," *Yale Classical Studies* 27 (1982), 28–59.

In verses twenty-seven and twenty-eight, the expression "God chose" is repeated thrice – God chose the foolish, God chose the weak things, God chose the despised and the insignificant. The theology of grace is significant in these verses (and in the whole pericope of 1 Cor 1:18–31) as God freely chooses to love those who are undeserving, which also shows the contrast between God and the world. "His love for the nobodies and the nothings discounted as nonentities and as insignificant in the value system of the world puts the world to shame by its reversal of judgement."[31] Paul here explains how the outsiders become the insiders in the eyes of the Lord and on the basis of the status derived from Christ (1 Cor 1:30–31).

Furthermore, in verse 28, the foolish things, weak things, and the insignificant things stand in contrast to the wise, strong, and those who have something as the phrase *ta onta* seems to suggest. On the other hand, the expression *ta mē onta* refers to things that are not, the despised, or best rendered as the "nothings" in two contexts: nothings in a socio-religious context and "somebody" and "something" in God's eyes. God brings down those who consider themselves to be significant in their own eyes. Horrell suggests that in the Roman society "one's value is determined by education, wealth, and breeding. The cross, on the other hand, turns the world upside down . . . a total transformation."[32] God subverts the value system in a society which measures people's worth according to socio-economic categories. The use of "idle" or "useless" *(argos)* is very powerful; it means utter zero put in relation to *ta me onta*, "to bring to nothing." As Barclay has rightly put it,

> *Worth is given by grace. Worth is relational and* it arises out of the relation of God to human beings – and it does not depend on inherent human properties or capacities. Worth in this understanding is imparted, bestowed, given – and it is given by the act of God in Jesus Christ.[33]

The worldly pattern of love is looking for what is good, pleasing, capable, talented, beautiful, and attractive, but the love of God in Christ is for those who are sinners, evil, ugly, unattractive, fools, and weak. The reason for this

---

31. Thiselton, *First Epistle to the Corinthians*, 184. There is a common feature between Paul and Jesus here. Jesus ate with those who were regarded by the society as "nobodies" in the sight of the "somebodies" in Jewish society. Furthermore, Jesus's parables were also related to the grace of the gospel which is in contrast with human criteria of worth.

32. D. G. Horrell, *The Social Ethos of the Corinthian Correspondence* (Edinburgh: T&T Clark, 1996), 134.

33. J. M. G. Barclay, "Paul, Grace and Liberation from Human Judgments of Worth," *The Mockingbird* 15 (2020), 53.

contrast is the grace of God bestowed on each and everyone to transform and make them good, pleasing, capable, and attractive in the sight of God. As grace means unmerited favour, grace always longs for a place which it can flow through, seeking the person, point, and need to achieve its purpose in this world of injustice, tension, and struggles. The love manifested in the cross of Christ seeks for the one unworthy, incapable, lowly, foolish, and weak, to transform this one into a new creation; to make "everything" new in order to make them worthy, capable, and strong. The process of transformation cannot be seen by anyone because it is invisible to human eyes.

The social status of *ta me onta* and *ta ischura* is striking in 1 Corinthians 1:26–31. It seems that these terms are more likely to refer to the physically disabled as weak, to the intellectually disabled as foolish, and having a despising attitude towards people who are disabled, regarding them as nothing. In other words, *ta me onta* seems to refer to: those who have intellectual disabilities; those who have no honour in the eyes of society; those who have no future in the sight of other people; those who are considered nothing by society; and those who are insignificant before others.

These people are not strong, clever, or talented and they may not possess any skills; nevertheless, God chooses them to become something. In other words, the person with disability has no identity of his own, but his identity is something acquired through the cross of Christ. God's free choice and grace have been poured upon them to shame those who are strong, those who are powerful, and those who are something. The weak, the foolish, and the dishonoured therefore stand in stark contrast to those who are strong and have good social status in the society. God exalts the lowly and humbles the proud in the Magnificat (Luke 1:51–52). He subverts the existing value systems; the purpose of God's free choice is that nobody should boast before him.

Within the typical Greco–Roman context, the Corinthians compete with each other; they are proud of the social status they have and envious of those with higher status.[34] Even slaves have their own status in their household.[35] Witherington suggests,

> The Corinthian people lived within an honour–shame orientation, where public recognition was often more important than facts, and where the worst thing that could happen was for one's

---

34. S. M. Pogoloff, *Logos and Sophia: The Rhetorical Structure of 1 Corinthians*, Society of Biblical Literature Dissertation Series 134 (Atlanta: Scholars, 1992), 211.

35. W. A. Meeks, *The Moral World of the First Christians* (Louisville: Westminster/ John Knox, 1986), 32–34.

reputation to be publicly tarnished. In such a culture a personal worth is based on recognition by others of one's accomplishments, hence the self-promoting.[36]

In their Greco-Roman society, dishonoured reputation, loss of face, the public humiliation which deprives the self of its social identity as a "someone" and reduces one to "nothing," and the pain of shame that follows public humiliation is a major social issue.

"Paul makes these negative points to highlight the glory of grace as sheer gift: God bestows self-acceptance and his own acceptance, setting aside guilt; he makes all kinds of people somethings or somebodies, setting aside shame."[37] The *dunatoi* (powerful) are people of social influence.[38] They have the influence and wealth to exert power in social and political realms. The Corinthians are competing with each other in a typical Greco–Roman context and they are proud of the social status they have and envious of those with higher status.[39] Even slaves have their own status in their household.[40] Here Paul is introducing a Christian tradition that everyone has a status in the Lord and cross subverting the human standards. On the basis of what we have received as a free gift, boasting is inappropriate before God. "Paul disrupts the intuitive status expectations of his audience by invoking a belief he knows they share: the belief that is in Christ, who was crucified, they have a common source of salvation and a common paradigm of leadership."[41]

Verses thirty and thirty-one define more clearly the gift we have in Jesus Christ – who became wisdom, righteousness, salvation, and redemption for the Corinthians. "In Christ" denotes sharing in Christ's own identity and becoming incorporated into Christ's body.[42] Being "in Christ" is not about showing an

---

36. Witherington, *Conflict and Community*, 8.

37. Thiselton, *First Epistle to the Corinthians*, 188.

38. Pogoloff, *Logos and Sophia*, 209.

39. Pogoloff, *Logos and Sophia*, 211.

40. W. A. Meeks, *The Moral World of the First Christians* (Louisville: Westminster/ John Knox, 1986), 32–34.

41. D. B. Martin, *The Corinthian Body* (New Haven: Yale University, 1995), 59.

42. Three phases mark the theology of being in Christ: 1) Deissmann speaks about the mystical aspect. G. A. Deissmann, *Paul: A Study in Social and Religious History* (Eng. trans. London: Hodder & Stoughton, 2nd ed., 1926), 161; 2) Weiss and Schweitzer point to the eschatological status of being in Christ as the mode of existence of God's new creation (J. Weiss, *Earliest Christianity: A History of the Period A.D. 30–150* (Cambridge: Peter Smith, 1970), 2:466; A. Schwietzer, *The Mysticism of Paul the Apostle*, trans. by W. Montgomery (London: Black, 1931, reprinted New York: Seabury, 1968), 26–40, 52–74. 3) Davies, Wilkenhauser, and Tannehill stress the derivative nature of the Christian experience resulting from the objective

individual's existence but sharing a state of belonging to the body of Christ. Here one finds the relevance of the person with disability as a member of the body of Christ (1 Cor 12and Rom 12). The implication of sharing in the body of Christ as limbs and members is sharing each other's sorrows and joys as "co-sufferer" and "co-wellbeing".[43] The four terms – wisdom, righteousness, sanctification, and redemption – are possibly related to the four terms – foolish things, weak things, the despised of no account, and the nothings (1 Cor 1:27–28). Bohatec relates and contrasts: a) wisdom and folly (divine action versus human achievement) b) weakness with righteousness (from lack of status to an accepted status) c) being despised with sanctification (God's chosen have the access to privileged places as one who belongs to them, and d) "nothings" with redemption, denoting a transference from a position of having no account to being one withdignity and freedom.[44] These fourqualities belong together; they characterise the act of Jesus Christ on the cross.

In 1 Corinthians 3:8 Paul refers to those who consider themselves to be wise. Divine wisdom is contrasted with human foolishness, which God will destroy. In a status-seeking society such as the one in Corinth

> wisdom is redefined and explicated as receiving the gifts of righteousness, sanctification and redemption freely bestowed through Christ and derivative from him. It is only that for Christian believers . Hence to glory in their newfound status as righteous, holy and redeemed is to glory in the Lord, and in no other person, no other thing. These other things are "nothings" not merely in a social sense, but in isolation from God, also in an ontological sense.[45]

Paul comes to the main point of his argument that "you are in Christ Jesus, who became to us wisdom from God, and righteousness and sanctification, and redemption, that just it is written 'Let him who boasts, boasts in the Lord'" (1 Cor 1:30–31). Society gives importance to the quality and quantity of beings, but God chooses those who are nothing in terms of quality and quantity. Paul

---

status of being in Christ. W. D. Davies, *Paul and Rabbinic Judaism: Some Rabbinic Elements in Pauline Theology* (London: SPCK, 2nd ed., 1958), 88; A. Wilkenhauser, *Pauline Mysticism* (New York: Herder, 1960); and Robert C. Tannehill, *Dying and Rising with Christ*, BZNW 32 (Berlin: Topelmann, 1966).

43. A. T. Robinson, *The Body: A Study in the Pauline Theology* (London: SCM, 1957), 51.

44. J. Bohatec, "Inhalt und Reihenfolge der 'Schlagworte der Erlösungsreligion' in 1 Kor 1:26–31" [Content and Order of the Keywords of the 'Religion of Salvation' in 1 Cor 1:26–31], 252–71. See also Thiselton, *First Epistle to the Corinthians*, 191.

45. Thiselton, *First Epistle to the Corinthians*, 192.

points to the formula "in the Lord" as marking the difference: Christ and the cross make the whole difference in the lives of those who are disabled.

Implication for the Person with Disability (1 Cor 2:1–7)

God has chosen those who are weak and despised. Paul's own experience in 1 Corinthians 2:1–7 illustrates well this point: he was with them in weakness, in fear, and in much trembling. His words were not excelling words of wisdom but came with a demonstration of the Spirit and of power. Here is a call for breakthrough in the attitude towards those who are at the margins of society – all societies – even though cultures, education standards, available technologies, etc., differ across countries and societies with attendant differences in attitudes and perspectives to disability. Paul's call for subverting the existing norms of society is remarkable and the tool he uses is the cross of Christ.

According to Amos Yong, Paul tries to distinguish between intellectual ability and intellectual disability.[46] Intellectual disability is a "general term and all-inclusive category that incorporates those congenitally affected, such as people with Down Syndrome, those who have brain injuries resulting in mental retardation and deficiency, and those who otherwise have cognitive dysfunctions of various sorts."[47] The major arguments of Yong's disability reading of 1 Corinthians 1:18–2:7 are as follows:[48]

1. The passage concerns divine wisdom and the wisdom of the age. He relates intellectual disability to the foolishness of God; the former may also embody the wisdom of God.

2. The Greek word *mōros* and its cognates are used five times in the first chapter of 1 Corinthians (1:20, 21, 23, 25, 27) (it is etymologically related to the English word *moron*). Paul says that morons are being redeemed by the gospel and shown to receive the saving power of God through the cross of Christ. Yong argues that, in such cases, morons, who are also the outcasts of society, may put to shame the wisdom of the world.

---

46. The names given for intellectual disability are idiot, imbecile, moron, retard, the feeble minded, mentally handicapped, those with cognitive or developmental disability, etc. The modern terms are differently abled, those with special needs, specific needs, etc. For a more detailed discussion, see Amos Yong, *Theology and Down Syndrome: Reimagining Disability in Late Modernity* (Waco: Baylor University, 2007), ch. 3.

47. A. Yong, *The Bible, Disability, and the Church: A New Vision of the People of God* (Grand Rapids: Eerdmans, 2011), 96. Intellectual disability is different from physical disability.

48. Yong, *Bible, Disability, and the Church*, 98.

3. In socio-rhetorical terms, the wisdom of the world refers to those who are powerful, influential, and part of the elite by birth or in other ways (1:26). The opposite group includes people of lower social strata who are weak, in shame, and have intellectual disabilities, both cognitive (lower intellectual capacity) and physical (in terms of power and capability).

    Paul refuses to boast regarding human wisdom, power, achievement, except in the Lord (1:31). His rhetorical claim may include those who have overcome the temptation of boasting; they have nothing to boast about or even do not know what they could boast about.

4. Paul speaks about God choosing the foolish (*mōra*) and the weak (*asthene*) of the world (1:27) but also the low and despised of the world, in other words, "things that are not" (1:28). He argues that the weak of the world include the infirm, the impaired, and the disabled, and thus, people with intellectual disabilities fit well in this category; they also fit well in the category of "things that are not." They "are doubly marginalised not only by the normate society but also by those with non-intellectual disabilities . . . If this is the case, then God's response to the wisdom of the world is the election of those people with intellectual disabilities."[49]

Yong formulates a theology of intellectual disability from 1 Corinthians 1:18–2:7. Paul told the Corinthians that he proclaims Christ crucified (1:23), and chooses to know nothing among them except Jesus Christ, and him crucified (2:3). Yong thinks that the "nothingness" characteristic of the lowliest and most despised of the world refers to people with intellectual disabilities and is a constitutive component of the message of the crucified Christ.[50] Paul connected his theology of weakness with the crucified Christ (2 Cor 13:4). Nevertheless, in 1 Corinthians, the argument is a bit broader in that Paul linked foolishness and the cross: "Christ crucified is the supreme symbol of the weakness and foolishness of God" and "the cross of Christ subverts the *normate* world."[51] According to Martin Albl, "In the ancient world, a crucified person was the

---

49. Yong, *Bible, Disability, and the Church*, 101.

50. Yong, *Bible, Disability, and the Church*, 101.

51. Yong, *Bible, Disability, and the Church*, 101. By normate biases Yong means the unexamined prejudices that a non-disabled people have towards disability and toward people who have them. These assumptions function normatively so that the inferior status of people with disabilities is inscribed into our consciousness.

ultimate example of 'disability.' A crucified person is with functional limitations and bore the ultimate in social stigmatisation."[52] Yong further explains that if ability, capability, and self-accomplishments are normate expectations, then disability, inability, and utter helplessness are symbols of the cross that represent God's power and wisdom. Thus, intellectual disability with its broad spectrum of physical limitations and mental impairments has its claim on the divine wisdom and power.

Paul interjects weakness in 1 Corinthians in a subversive manner that turns the normate assumptions upside down. Weakness should no longer be seen in a derogatory and exclusionary way. In a surprising move, he shows how God relocates the weak from the periphery to the centre of his works. The biased and discriminatory effects of wisdom and the hierarchical and oppressive forms of power are challenged head on as God uses the foolish and weak in surprising ways to make them conduits of his grace and glory. In the light of our preceding reflections, it could be very well established that the weak includes people with different forms of disabilities.

---

52. Martin Albl, "'For Whenever I am Weak, Then I am Strong': Disability in Paul's Epistles," in *This Abled Body: Rethinking Disabilities in Biblical Studies*, eds. Hector Avalos, Sarah J. Melcher and Jeremy Schipper (Atlanta: Society of Biblical Literature, 2007), 149.

4

The Person with Disability in the Body of Christ

The Spiritual Gifts and Talents of the Persons with Disability

Persons with disability are the creation of God and they are part of the body of Christ. So, what should be our attitude towards their spiritual gifts and receiving ministry from them? Diversity grounded in unity is the major theme of 1 Corinthians 12. Paul emphasises unity in diversity in order to overcome divisions on the basis of the gifts apportioned to the believers in the Corinthian church. Martin suggests that "in 12:4–11 Paul continually stresses unity in diversity in order to overcome divisiveness owing to various valuations being assigned to different gifts, with tongues as the implied higher-status gift."[1] The different gifts, ministries, and activities are apportioned by the same Spirit, same Lord, and the same God (12:4–6). Unity is important and diversity is secondary to the unity. Gifts are given with a purpose or goal of "building" the body (12:11). The one source is the Spirit and God gives the gifts graciously through Christ and the Spirit. The word *diaireō* occurs in 1 Corinthians 12:4 and Luke 15:12, twice in the New Testament and means either differences, distinctions, or apportioning. Paul's change of the Corinthian word *pneumatika* "spiritual things" to *charismata* "spiritual gifts" points towards the gift of grace given to different people, as Conzelmann puts it, "God's generous act of freely apportioning different gifts to different recipients."[2]

God's grace through the cross is active in ecclesiology and ministry. The Corinthians used *pneumatikon* for a wide range of religious feeling states and observable phenomenon. But Paul redefines "spiritual" as what God freely

---

1. Martin, *Corinthian Body*, 87.
2. Conzelmann, *1 Corinthians*, 207.

gives, in his initiative, and in his own sovereign choice (12:11) as empowerments (12:6) through the agency of the Holy Spirit for the practical service of God and other people (12:5). The word charisma is repeatedly used in 1 Corinthians 12:4, 9, 28, 30, 31 and Romans 12:6.

Most striking is the use of the word "same" in this passage. The same Spirit is apportioning gifts in different believers and the giver is significant separately to the gift. "The same gift distributes more of the Holy Spirit because he has more gifts. The same Spirit distributes the small or the large gift, not because he favours one Christian less or more than the other, but because of His sovereign purposes."[3] Furthermore, God is the ultimate source of spiritual activities and it is he who activates them in everyone (12:6). Thus, gifts are given for serving (*diakoniōn*) and not for boasting. Different ministries are associated with the same Lord; under his lordship each Christian has to obey, trust, and serve as a slave.[4] The same Spirit apportions gifts in different ways and according to divine purposes, and the same Lord commissions various ways of serving.[5] Gifts, services, and workings are not different entities or different experiences, but different ways of looking at what are called "manifestations of the Spirit" by Paul (12:7). The work of the same God brings everything in everyone. "It is not a self-induced activity but an activity activated by God."[6] Calvin refers this to the grace of God: "Men have nothing good or praiseworthy except what comes from God alone."[7] "The unity and grace of God as one, who nevertheless dispenses his gifts in variety through Christ as the Lord by the Holy Spirit calls attention to God as "author, authoriser, destiny and judge . . . (Rom 12:1–2; 13:1–4; 1 Thess 4:3; 1 Cor 6:13–14; 8:6; 12:4–6)."[8] Here God is present as the bestower of gifts to everyone according to his grace and the person with disability is not omitted from the bestowal. God the Father works as he wills, and the Spirit and the Lord are also active in the manifestation of the gifts.

Lists of gifts occur in three of Paul's epistles (Rom 12:6–8; 1 Cor 12:8–11; 12:27–28; and Eph 4:11). Dunn, on the basis of the different lists, differentiates gifts to miracles, revelation, inspired speech, and service, all because of the

---

3. S. Zodhiates, *1 Corinthians 12* (Chattanooga: AMG, 1983), 1, 68–69.
4. C. K. Barrett, *The First Epistle to the Corinthians* (London: A. & C. Black, 1968), 284.
5. G. Deluz, *A Companion to 1 Corinthians* (London: DLT, 1963), 172.
6. Thiselton, *First Epistle to the Corinthians*, 933.
7. J. Calvin, *The First Epistle of Paul the Apostle to the Corinthians* (Edinburgh: Oliver & Boyd, 1960), 261.
8. Thiselton, *First Epistle to the Corinthians*, 934.

divine grace; "charisma is always an event, the gracious activity of God through Christ."[9] The named gifts in 1 Corinthians 12:8–11 (NRSV) are:

a. Utterance of wisdom
b. Utterance of knowledge
c. Faith
d. Gifts of healing
e. Working of miracles
f. Prophecy
g. Discernment of spirits
h. Various kinds of tongues
i. Interpretation of tongues

Utterance of Wisdom and Knowledge

The utterance of wisdom is concerned with an utterance derived from God's wisdom or about God's wisdom. Wisdom (*sophia*) is a catch word in the Corinthian community and used sixteen times in 1 Corinthians (1:17, 19, 20, 21, 22, 24, 30; 2:1, 4, 5, 6, 7, 13; 3:19). Paul is addressing a community that seeks human wisdom (1:17–22; 2:1–5; 3:19) and the gift of divine wisdom (1:24–31; 2:6–13). Kistemaker suggests that "the gift is the ability to speak divine wisdom which believers receive through the Holy Spirit (compare 2:6–7). Paul contrasts this divine wisdom with human wisdom (1:17, 20, 25)."[10]

Wisdom here is related to God's grace and the cross of Christ. It is a part of the response to grace.[11] Wisdom is a shared experience; it relates to God's plan of salvation, namely, his saving act on the cross through Christ, and is intended for the building up of the church (1:26–31). "Wisdom relates to building up the community for the *common advantage of all* through appropriation of the power and lifestyle of Christ."[12] The first two gifts according to Craig refer to

---

9. J. D. G. Dunn, *Jesus and the Spirit: A Study of the Religious and Charismatic Experience of Jesus and the First Christians as Reflected in the New Testament* (London: SCM, 1965), 201–58, at 254.

10. S. J. Kistemaker, 1 Corinthians NTC (Grand Rapids: Baker Books, 1993), 421.

11. J. A. Davis, *Wisdom and Spirit* (Lanham: University Press of America, 1984), 71–149.

12. Thiselton, *First Epistle to the Corinthians*, 940 (italics original).

the teaching ministries of the church.[13] It is difficult to distinguish between the utterance of wisdom and knowledge; the former relates to the divine wisdom and the latter refers to the knowledge of God or being known by God against the epistemology of the Gnostics. Thistleton describes how:

> Augustine observes that for Paul "in Christ Jesus are hidden all the treasures of wisdom and knowledge" (Col 2:3); hence in 1 Corinthians 12:8, although wisdom may relate to "divine things" and "knowledge to human things" both aspects concern the believer's relationship to Christ, activated through the Spirit."[14]

While some regard Augustine's stance as relating wisdom to the eternal realities and knowledge to the temporal things, Dunn suggests that the "utterance of knowledge" may be understood as "a word spoken under inspiration giving an insight into cosmic realities and relationships."[15] Furthermore, Thiselton states that the "gift of *articular* communicative *utterance* may draw on *wisdom* and *knowledge* from God especially when this serves both 'the common good' of all and the proclamation of the cross."[16]

Faith and Various Kinds of Healings

The reference to faith in the list of spiritual gifts does not refer to saving faith since the Spirit apportions this gift to someone who is distinct from the majority of believers (*heteros*). Bruce suggests that the faith here concerns "a special endowment of faith for a special service" (compare 1 Cor 13:2b).[17] The faith here can be related to the faith illustrated in Hebrews 11:6–29 and the faith to move mountains (Matt 17:20; 1 Cor 13:2). This faith is linked with various kinds of healing, which do not appear in the lists mentioned in Romans or Ephesians.

The specific noun *iama* (healing) occurs only here in the New Testament (12:9, 28, 30), although the verb occurs in other books of the New Testament. Paul refers to healing only here in 1 Corinthians except his explicit mention in 2 Corinthians 12:8, where he mentions praying three times for the removal of

---

13. C. T. Craig, *The First Epistle to the Corinthians*, IB, 10 (New York: Nashville: Abingdon, 1953), 3–262, at 151.

14. Augustine, *On the Trinity*, 13: (19) 24, cited by Thiselton, *First Epistle to the Corinthians*, 941.

15. Dunn, *Jesus and the Spirit*, 218.

16. Thiselton, *First Epistle to the Corinthians*, 944 (emphasis original).

17. F. F. Bruce, *1 and 2 Corinthians*, NCBC (London: Oliphants, 1971), 119.

the thorn in his flesh, "but rather than a charisma of healing God gave him his grace as his sufficiency leaving his weakness without special healing."[18] Furthermore, the gift of healing comes within God's sovereign choice, for example, Paul's request for healing was finally decided by God. The plural "kinds" used here "denotes various kinds of healings enacted in a diversity of ways to address a variety of conditions, and not a uniform stereotypical ministry performed by a permanently endowed 'healer.'"[19] An Anglican statement rightly suggests

> All true wholeness, health, and healing come from God. We do not therefore regard "divine healing" as being always miraculous. We also look forward to the resurrection, knowing that only then shall we be finally and fully freed from sickness, weakness, pain, and mortality. At the same time, we welcome the recovery by the Church of a concern for healing . . . but also wish to express caution against giving wrong impressions and causing unnecessary distress through (i) making it appear as it is sinful for a Christian to be ill; (ii) laying too great a stress and responsibility upon the faith of the individual who is seeking healing.[20]

Working of Miracles

Although in the New Testament many of the healings are miraculous in nature, and Paul specifically mentions about healing as a separate gift, the gift of working of miracles would be something other than physical healing. They are mighty works of power or *dunamis*. This means that the term may refer to any kind of activity where God's mighty power is evident.[21] It may include deliverance from physical danger (as in the deliverance of the apostles from prison in

---

18. Thiselton, *First Epistle to the Corinthians*, 947.

19. Thiselton, *First Epistle to the Corinthians*, 948. Thisleton cites the following commentaries: F. L. Godet, *Commentary on the First Epistle of St. Paul to the Corinthians*, vol. 2, chs. 9–16. trans. by A. Cusin (Edinburgh: T&T Clark, 1887), 197; H. A. W. Meyer, *Critical and Exegetical Handbook to the Epistles to the Corinthians* (Eng. trans. 2 vols. Edinburgh: T&T Clark, 1892) (vol. 1 and vol. 2, 1–124 on 1 Corinthians), 1:364; A. T. Robertson and A. Plummer, *A Critical and Exegetical Commentary on the First Epistle of St. Paul to the Corinthians*, ICC (Edinburgh: T&T Clark, 1914), 266; H. L. Goudge, *The First Epistle to the Corinthians*, 3rd ed. Westminster Commentaries (London: Methuen, 1911), 110.

20. Anglican Church, "Gospel and Spirit: A Joint Statement," in McDonnell (ed.), *Presence, Power and Praise: Documents on the Charismatic Renewal* (Collegeville: Liturgical Press, 1980), 2:305.

21. Wayne Grudem, *Systematic Theology: An Introduction to Biblical Doctrine* (Secunderabad: OM Books, 2003), 1062.

Acts 5:19–20 or 12:6–11),[22] or powerful works of judgement on the unfaithful Christians or enemies of the gospel such as Ananias or Elymas[23] (Acts 5:1–11; 13:9–12). But such acts of spiritual power may also include power to triumph over demonic opposition (Acts 16:18).

However, it is to be noted that deeds of power need not always be looked at as spectacular displays of power. As Thiselton points out,

> But in and through the cross, **power** and even **deeds of power**, became transposed into that which made actively effective the loving and salvific purposes of the heart of God, as revealed in Christ's acceptance of constraints and renunciation of force and spectacle in his messianic temptations.[24]

The crucified and risen Christ, "bestows through the Spirit a gift of victory which may draw its power *both from the pattern and reality of the cross* (with all its constraints and 'weakness') and from the pattern and reality of the resurrection."[25]

Prophecy

The gift of prophecy in the New Testament refers to a spiritual gift bestowed by the Holy Spirit upon believers. What is prophecy? According to Gordon Fee, "prophecy consisted of spontaneous, Spirit-inspired, intelligible messages, orally delivered in the gathered assembly."[26] In the New Testament, as Bittlinger points out, prophecy is not in the first instance foretelling (prediction of future) but rather forth-telling (proclamation).[27] In continuation with prophecy in the Old Testament, prophets may often allude to past and to future events insofar as they shed light on the present or entail promise as a basis for present action or understanding.

New Testament prophecy emphasizes building up the church and helping believers grow in their faith. Prophecy, as a gift of the Holy Spirit, combines pastoral insight into the needs of persons, communities and situations with the ability to address these with a God-given utterance or longer discourse leading

---

22. Grudem, *Systematic Theology*, 1062.
23. Thiselton, *First Epistle to the Corinthians*, 954.
24. Thiselton, *First Epistle to the Corinthians*, 954. Emphasis original.
25. Thiselton, *First Epistle to the Corinthians*, 956. Emphasis original.
26. Gordon D. Fee, *God's Empowering Presence: The Holy Spirit in the Letters of Paul* (Grand Rapids: Baker Books, 2009), 170.
27. *The Holy Spirit in the Letters of Paul* (Grand Rapids: Baker Books, 2009), 42.

to challenge or comfort, judgment or consolation but ultimately building up the addressees.[28] Paul says in 1 Corinthians 14:3 that this gift is given for the common good of the church, intended to strengthen, encourage, and comfort believers. The exercise of this gift is to be done with humility, discernment, and in accordance with biblical teachings, under the guidance of the Holy Spirit and subject to the authority of Scripture.

Discernment of Spirits

> The gift of discernment of spirits is mentioned in 1 Corinthians 12:10, where Paul lists various spiritual gifts given by the Holy Spirit for the common good of the church. Grudem defines it as a special ability to recognize the influence of the Holy Spirit or of demonic spirits in a person.[29]

In several instances, Jesus discerned the presence of evil spirits and cast them out (e.g., Mark 1:23–27). Paul discerns that a slave girl's ability to predict the future is due to a spirit of divination, and he commands the spirit to leave her (Acts 16:16–18). Discernment of spirits involves distinguishing between the Holy Spirit, human spirit and demonic spirit. Hence there is a need for Christians to "test the spirits to whether they are of God; for many false prophets have gone out into the world" (1 John 4:1).

Sometimes the presence of demonic activity is outwardly evident, and some other times in the form of false doctrines (1 Cor 12:2–3; 1 John 4:1–6). It may also manifest through violent and bizarre physical actions, especially in the face of Christian preaching (Mark 1:24; 9:20).[30] But in addition to these outward indications of demonic influence, there is probably also a more subjective perception that occurs at the spiritual and emotional level, whereby the presence of demonic activity is distinguished.[31] Understanding and exercising the gift of discernment of spirits involves humility, wisdom, and reliance on God. It is essential for the health and protection of the church and the spiritual growth of its members.

---

28. Thiselton, *First Epistle to the Corinthians*, 964.
29. Grudem, *Systematic Theology*, 1082.
30. Grudem, *Systematic Theology*, 1083.
31. Grudem, *Systematic Theology*, 1083.

Various kinds of Tongues and Interpretation

The gifts of different kinds of tongues and interpretation should be considered together because of their interrelation. Tongues is the ability given by the Holy Spirit to speak in a language not understood by the speaker. It could be prayer or praise addressed to God. On the day of Pentecost disciples began to speak in other tongues, as the Spirit gave them utterance (Acts 2:4). People who gathered there from different territories could understand their speech as each one heard them speaking in his own language (Acts 2:6). However, at other times, the speech will be in a language that no one understands (1 Cor 14:2).

Paul distinguishes between the private and public use of tongues. Speaking in tongues causes edification of the individual, as it is directed to God as praise or prayer. But in the case of the public use of tongues the church does not profit if there is no interpreter, and one who has a gift of tongues should keep silent in church and speak themselves to God (1 Cor 14:28). However, if there is exhortation in tongues followed by interpretation, that would be equivalent to prophecy as it would edify the congregation. The spiritual gifts are bestowed by God upon, and exercised by, the body of Christ and its members for the common good of both the church and the world.

This perspective makes better sense, then, of Paul's linking the charismata to ecclesiology, in particular his emphasis on the diversity of members as including the indispensability of those who are thought to be weaker (1 Cor 12:22). In fact, not only are these presumably weaker members essential, but they are to be "treated with greater respect" and honor (12:23b, 24b) and all members ought to "have the same care for one another" (12:25b). Notice here two important truths. First, the apparently weaker members also have gifts, and thus gifts are not signs of superiority as defined by the world's conventions. Second, any expression of the gifts, even by those deemed more honorable, are not for their own commendation but for the sake of others.

I address here two questions: spiritual gifts and ministry from the person with disability, and ministry to the person with disability. Often people are reluctant to receive ministry from the person with disability because of prejudices about illness. In a church in Durham, UK, we received communion from a lady in a wheelchair. If God has given the gift of praying/prophecy to a person with disability, we should accept it from that person since the same Spirit has endowed the gift. If God has graciously apportioned a gift to the person with disability, it should be accepted, as the gift is for the common benefit. In other words, persons with disability or with abled-bodies are both members of the body of Christ.

The weaker members of the body cannot be excluded from being channels of the Spirit's manifestation. God freely distributes the Spirit's charisms to all members of the body so that each one can contribute to the common good of the body. The gifts are not only given to stronger members in order to minister to the weaker members; the gifts of the Spirit are manifest through all members of the body, regardless of their ability or disability. It is God the Spirit who chooses the recipients of the charismata and there is a multiplicity of recipients as there is a variety of body members.

The one body of Christ is constituted by people across the spectrum of dis/abilities. The Spirit distributes many gifts to many members, and gifts are essential for the whole church body to be built up and edified. The weaker-bodied and more abled-bodied members are equally necessary for the health of the whole church. No gift and no individual believer needs to be suppressed, minimised, or discriminated against and there is no hierarchy of gifts.[32] Therefore all gifts are equally indispensable, and each person is equally important for the health of the whole. People with disabilities are therefore essential for healthy and functioning congregations.

Amos Yong has woven these insights into the following outline for an inclusive ecclesiology, which is given with additional reflection from my part.

1. The church is constituted first and foremost of the weak, not the strong; people with disabilities are thus at the centre rather than at the margins of what it means to be the people of God. It provides a new vision of what is meant by the "people of God."

2. Each person with disability contributes something essential to and for the body through his or her presence and activity. People with disabilities are therefore ministers empowered by the Spirit of God, each one in his or her own specific ways, rather than merely recipients of the ministries of the non-disabled people. A mutually enriching and edifying ministry would be liberative of the experience of people with disability and at the same time would be true to the understanding of the "universal priesthood of all believers."

3. People with disabilities become the paradigm for embodying the power of God and manifesting the divine glory. This understanding can make a shift from stigmatisation of disability to acknowledging its significance in the context of God's purpose. We should be cautious against sentimentalizing or valorising weakness. What we

---

32. Yong, *Bible, Disability, and the Church*, 96.

should do is to honour the diversity of the body's members, with and without disabilities without over-emphasizing either abilities or disabilities. Thus, in light of Paul's ecclesiology, our understanding of strong and weak and ability and disability will be transformed.

The Person with Disability in the Body of Christ: 1 Cor 12:12–31

Paul uses the body metaphor to deal with the Corinthians' erroneous view of spiritual gifts that affects their social harmony (1 Cor 12:12–31). Paul's use of the body metaphor in 1 Corinthians is important to the present analysis since: a) it is an elaborate description of the body metaphor; b) Paul's portrayal here is more descriptive than in Romans; and c) it helps to identify the place of the disabled in the body of Christ.

One Body, Many Members (12:12, 13)

The "one body" is characterised by many members. In spite of its variety of members, it is nevertheless one body. Paul uses two comparative particles "for just . . . so also" and he applies the metaphor to Christ and not to the church (1 Cor 12:12).[33] Garland suggests that "the clause 'so also is Christ' is awkward only because Christ is shorthand for the church as the body of Christ (12:27)."[34] Nevertheless, this notion is challenged as it would imply "the ontological identification between Christ and the church."[35] In the same vein, Barrett argues that such identification is unthinkable for Paul since Jesus is the Lord of all the church (12:3). Furthermore, he observes, "Christ however remains always as the prototype of the relationship."[36]

---

33. In Col 1:18, the church is called Christ's body. The same comparative particles are repeated in Rom 12:4–5. Although Paul repeats the same subject to the Roman believers, the passage is shorter than in 1 Corinthians.

34. D. E. Garland, *1 Corinthians* (BECNT, Grand Rapids: Baker Academic, 2003), 590. Fee supports the view that "Christ means the church as a shortened form for the body of Christ." G. D. Fee, *The First Epistle to the Corinthians* (Grand Rapids: Eerdmans, 1987), 602.

35. Thiselton, *First Epistle to the Corinthians*, 996. The following verses 12:12–30 do not support this view (Best and Whitley). Käsemann observes: "Ecclesiological metaphysics are read even into the Pauline statements in a highly dangerous way . . . to put the matter somewhat too epigrammatically, the apostle is not interested in the church per se . . . He is only interested in it so far as it is the means whereby Christ reveals himself on the earth and becomes incarnate in the world through his spirit. E. Käsemann, "The Theological Problem Presented by the Motif of the Body of Christ," in *Perspectives on Paul* (London: SCM, 1971), 102–21 at 110, 117.

36. C. K. Barrett, *The First Epistle to the Corinthians* (London: A. & C. Black, 1968), 286.

Paul aims to urge unity or oneness among the Corinthian believers. He proposes that although the body is one, it has many members and (equally and conversely) although there are many members, it is one. In 1 Corinthians 10:17, the idea that many are one body is drawn from the concept of the Lord's table, with many of them eating of the one loaf. Best suggests that this is what Paul will argue from and not argue for.[37] Paul further emphasises that the body can function only through its diversified members. Therefore, there can be diversity in unity and unity in diversity. For just as the body has many limbs and organs and yet they make up one body, so also the body of Christ despite its various organs and differing functions, makes one body. Although uniformity cannot be expected in different organs and limbs that constitute a body, there can be unity in plurality. Soards observes, "Paul's point is unity dominates diversity and makes diversity genuinely meaningful and constructive" rather than simply unity in diversity and diversity in unity.[38]

Diversity of Members (12:14–20)

Paul affirms that diversity is part and parcel of the body as he compares one sense organ with another, using the classical rhetorical technique of personification (12:15–16). As Thiselton suggests,

> It is precisely not a late twentieth-century or early twenty-first century "postmodern" assurance that within certain boundaries everyone "does one's own thing." The respective functions of hands, feet (v. 15), ears, and eyes (v. 16) coordinate the organism as one. If each did not play his or her assigned role, the one body would collapse into a chaotic non-entity. Hence, v. 15 not only reassures those who feel inferior that they do indeed belong to the body, but also asserts the necessity for the coherent unity of the body both of those who feel inferior and to those who devalue others.[39]

Since the "many" are expected to perform their assigned and different roles, the body is a differentiated entity, that is, plurality and diversity of the body is

---

37. Best, *Body,* 96. Best's reading of 1 Corinthians 12 in the whole context of 1 Corinthians 12–14 is unsatisfactory. See Fee, *First Epistle to the Corinthians,* 602.

38. M. L. Soards, *1 Corinthians* (NIBC, Peabody: Hendrickson, 1999), 263.

39. Thiselton, *First Epistle to the Corinthians,* 1002. The protasis of the conditional sentence uses an aorist subjunctive: ἐὰν εἴπῃ ὁ πούς and means "if the foot should say" or "if the foot were to say" (NJB) or "suppose the foot were to say" (REB), and the apodosis: οὐκ εἰμὶ ἐκ τοῦ σώματος "I am not of the body" or "I do not belong to the body" (NRSV, REB, NIV, NJB).

emphasised (12:14). Paul uses double negatives in verses fifteen and sixteen so that the result becomes positive: "if the foot should say, 'because I am not a hand, I do not belong to the body'; if the ear should say, 'because I am not an eye, I do not belong to the body.'" The foot and the hand despite their difference belong to the body, the same with the eye and the ear. Difference does not indicate that the physical bodily organs are independent. Similarly, there are different spiritual gifts and those are to be used as being parts of one spiritual body.

Another type of rhetorical question is asked by Paul in verse seventeen regarding the members that belong to the physical body in pairs. The question seems to be like a chain: eye/hearing, hearing/smell, etc. The absence of a single member makes the body deficient; in other words, if the parts of the body that are necessary are lacking, it certainly hinders the body's proper functioning. The message here is clearly addressing those who see themselves as inferior and this also seems to be a logical move to challenge those who assume that they are the ones who make the whole (body) as it is. Therefore, each different task is essential and crucial for the proper functioning of the body.

The members of the body are properly arranged so that each one has its own place (12:18). The phrase *nuni de* expresses the logical "now then." As Garland suggests, "it introduces the real situation after an unreal conditional clause: 'but as a matter of fact,' God made the body with its intricately interconnected parts so that it could perform at its optimum in the world."[40] In the traditional Hellenistic use of the body metaphor, each one has its own place and the harmonious order in the body is derived from nature. Paul affirms that God has arranged the organs of the body as he willed (*kathōs ethelēsen*) (1 Cor 12:18; compare 12:11). Fee observes that the emphasis is not on the orderly arrangement of the body; rather it is more likely on the "divine placement" of each member.[41] As Thiselton suggests,

> to try to rank some gifts as "more essential" than others, let alone as necessary marks of advanced status to which all should aspire, is to offer a blasphemous challenge to God's freedom to choose whatever is his good will for his people both collectively and individually.[42]

---

40. Garland, *1 Corinthians*, 595.

41. Fee, *First Epistle to the Corinthians*, 611. He refers back to vv. 7–11, where the spirit gives the various manifestations to "each person just as he pleases." In vv. 24–27, Paul emphasizes that being "many parts of the one body" is God's design.

42. Thiselton, *First Epistle to the Corinthians*, 1004.

It is evident from verse twenty that the body cannot exist if all the members are the same (in other words, without diversity). We also find in this verse a thematic echo of 1 Corinthians 12:17: "If the whole body were an eye, where would be the hearing?" As Fee suggests, "If all the parts were of one kind, there would be no body at all, only a monstrosity! The concern for diversity can scarcely be missed."[43]

Paul sums up the argument in 1 Corinthians 12:20, following on from what he has made already clear – the body should have many members. *Mele* is rendered as "members" (NRSV) and as "limbs" and "organs" (REB); the latter should be preferred since *mele* has a more specific physical sense than the word "members" would suggest. *Men* and *de* are translated as "on the one hand . . . on the other hand." Hence, it seems that 1 Corinthians 12:20 may have the force of an axiom: many limbs and organs (on one side) and the body (on the other). Nevertheless, Barrett interprets it as a fact rather than an axiom by translating: "but in fact there are many members and one body."[44] Thus, Paul has made clear that both diversity and unity are necessary aspects of a body (that is, unity in diversity and diversity in unity). Afterwards, he proceeds to emphasise the interdependence of its different parts.

The Need for Interdependence (v. 21)

Paul explicitly states what he wants to convey by the rhetoric of the body. As Thiselton observes, "not only does the rhetoric of the body reassure those with supposedly 'inferior' or 'dispensable' gifts that they do indeed belong fully to the body as essential limbs and organs, but *this rhetoric now explicitly rebukes those who think that they and their 'superior' gifts are self-sufficient for the whole body, or that others are scarcely 'authentic' parts of the body, as they themselves are.*"[45] He continues,

> No subset of gifts or experience constitutes the *esse* of the church, any more than some selected form of ministerial office represents the *esse* of the church. Both the *esse* and the *bene esse* lie in

---

43. Fee, *First Epistle to the Corinthians*, 611.

44. Barrett, First *Epistle to the Corinthians*, 290; F. Godet, *First Epistle to the Corinthians* (CFTL New Series, Vol. XXX; Edinburgh: T&T Clark, 1898), 2:214. Godet interprets this as an "actual fact." It is a concise epigram as suggested by Meyer, Robertson and Plummer; H. A. W. Meyer, *Critical and Exegetical Handbook to the Epistles to the Corinthians: First Epistle* (Edinburgh: T&T Clark, 1892), 1:376; A. Robertson and A. Plummer, *A Critical and Exegetical Commentary on the First Epistle of Paul to the Corinthians* (Edinburgh: T&T Clark, 1914), 274.

45. Thiselton, *First Epistle to the Corinthians*, 1005 (Italics original).

the mutual respect for, and acceptance of, what God has chosen (12:11) as that which promotes the Lordship of Christ (12:3) and the building up of the church for the common good (12:7), in an equality of *status* of those who owe their being in Christ to the gracious agency of the Holy Spirit as a gift for **all** (12:13).[46]

It is clear that a single gift cannot be used to evaluate other believers. Furthermore, Paul describes self-sufficiency as "having no need" of others, and thus, this has nothing to do with the attitude of Christ. Paul compares the different organs of the body to the diverse gifts, emphasising the fact that they are "for the common good" (1 Cor 12:7) and the diversity is so essential that no organ can say that "I have no need of you" (1 Cor 12:21). The method of personification is employed by Paul as he pictures an imaginary dialogue between the different parts of the body, the eye, the hand, the head, the feet (compare 12:15–16) and suggests that some of the Corinthian believers think they are the essential members of the body. In connection to this, Garland suggests that "eye" and "head" mean those in leadership roles, while "the hands" and "feet" represent the slaves or the labouring class.[47] Thus, Paul asserts that the body has many members and these several members are interdependent to each other, meaning that each organ needs the other to exist.

Honouring the Less Honourable

In 1 Corinthians 12:22–24a, Paul speaks about the honourable and the less honourable members of the body in order to demonstrate the need for interdependence. He uses the word *asthenestera*, which is the comparative form of the adjective *asthenēs*, to denote the weaker members.[48] Theissen and others consider it as referring to those with lower social status, whereas for Glad it denotes "dispositions of character . . . psychological dispositions or character

---

46. Thiselton, *First Epistle to the Corinthians*, 1006 (Italics original). *Esse* is a Latin word meaning essence.

47. Garland, *1 Corinthians*, 595. See Fee, *First Epistle to the Corinthians*, 610–11; D. G. Horrell, *The Social Ethos of the Corinthian Correspondence: Interest and Ideology from 1 Corinthians to 1 Clement* (Edinburgh: T&T Clark, 1996), 179–80.

48. τὸ ἀσθενὲς τοῦ θεοῦ ("the weakness of God," 1 Cor 1:25); τὰ ἀσθενῆ τοῦ κόσμου ("the weak of the world," 1 Cor 1:27), where the weak are the goal of God's election. The distinction between the strong and the weak (4:10) and the relation between them (8:7, 9, 10) were discussed earlier in the letter.

types revealing aptitudes . . . and . . . maturity."[49] The common understanding of "weak" (*asthenēs*) has changed in the wake of the challenging thoughts of Glad and Martin. As Thiselton suggests,

> Paul refers to people in the church whose role, or more probably temperament, or perhaps both, present them as **less endowed with power or status than others**. The "strong" or the "gifted" perceived them as not providing much effective *weight or power* in the church's mission, and not much *confidence* borne of *status*. They were insufficiently impressive to count for much, either socially or spiritually, within the church, or in terms of what "contacts" or ability they might show for mission or for speaking with wisdom and knowledge to outsiders. Probably they never did effective mighty works or healing, seldom or never prophesied, and perhaps never spoke in tongues.[50]

Before drawing attention to the unpresentable parts of the body (12:23), Paul states that the parts of the body which are less endowed with power and status are essential (*anankaios*, 12:22). Possibly, Paul calls the less endowed "essential parts" since the strong and the gifted perceive themselves as the "core of the church." Thus, it is worth quoting Chrysostom here:

> What is meaner than the foot? What is more honourable than the head? For this, the head, more than anything, is the man. Nevertheless . . . it could not do everything on its own . . . The greater have need of the less . . . For nothing . . . is dishonourable, seeing it is God's work.[51]

---

49. C. E. Glad, *Paul and Philodemus: Adaptability in Epicurean and Early Christian Psychology* (NovTSup, 81; Leiden: Brill, 1995), 333. Glad suggests that it does not refer to the social or spiritual status of people or to their "theological positions." In NRSV, NIV, NJB, and JB, *asthenēs* is translated as weaker or weakest, but in RV "more feeble" and in REB "more frail" are used. These translations can hardly be followed as per the suggestions of Glad and Martin in terms of "disposition of character." See Thiselton, *First Epistle to the Corinthians*, 1006.

50. Thiselton, *First Epistle to the Corinthians*, 1007 (Emphasis and italics original). Fee suggests that Paul has in mind the internal organs, which are weaker, but protected internally. It is striking that they "seem" to be weaker and need not necessarily be so. If an organ is removed because of its weakness, it affects the wholeness of the body. All parts, even if they are weaker, make the body whole. See Fee, *First Epistle to the Corinthians*, 613.

51. Chrysostom, *Hom.* 1 Cor 31:1, 2. Other Church fathers also applied the idea that the believers need to give care, protection, and support to those who are in need in order to follow the footsteps of Christ in serving others. See D. Bonhoeffer, *Christology* (Eng. trans., London: SCM, 1978); *The Communion of the Saints: A Dogmatic Inquiry into the Sociology of the Church* (Eng. trans., New York: Harper & Row, 1963), and *Ethics* (New York: Macmillan, 1965); J. Calvin,

Paul speaks to a society where shame and honour are values and forces, whereas these are less emphasised in our contemporary society. He refers to the reversal of status of the weaker, less honourable, and more shameful members of the body. Thus, he concludes that the unpresentable parts are given more honour than the presentable parts.[52] The word *peritithemen* is translated as "invest," since it could be understood in two senses, as bestowing or conferring (Prov 12:9, LXX) or as putting a garment around (Matt 27:28; Mark 15:17). Therefore the unpresentable parts are bestowed with more honour, which challenges the normal hierarchy of values that honour the privileged and humiliate those who are poor in society. In other words, Paul envisages here a reversal of status- the lower being made higher and vice versa; a parallel paradox can be found in the cross of the Christ.[53] Those who assume that they are gifted because of their knowledge and wisdom are far from being the essence of the church. Moltmann argues that "the disabled constitute a gift of the Spirit to the church through the offering of weakness."[54] Paul notes that the church is Christ's limbs and members and those that "the church likes to put 'on display' as our 'best' people (whether because of their supposed wisdom and knowledge, or more visible gifts of the Spirit such as tongues or 'mighty works') are far from being the essence of the church."[55] The church constitutes not only people who are gifted, wise, and strong but also those who are in need, poor, meek, persecuted, and those who mourn (Matt 5:3–10). Those who seek status in the church are in a way having the same spirit as those in the secular Corinth. Here, there is a twist and a shift from such type of attitude. Thus, as Bonhoeffer states, blessed are those

> refusing to be in tune with the world, or to accommodate oneself to its standards. Such men mourn for the world . . . While the world keeps holiday they stand aside . . . they mourn . . . The world dreams of progress, of power and of the future . . . No wonder

---

The First Epistle of Paul the Apostle to the Corinthians (Edinburgh: Oliver & Boyd, 1960), 268; M. Luther, *Early Theological Works* (trans. & ed. J. Atkinson) (London: SCM, 1962), 290–94.

52. Martin notes that "the genitals may seem to be the most shameful part of the body, but our very attention to them – our constant care to cover them and shield them from trivializing and vulgarizing public exposure – demonstrates that they are actually the most necessary of the body's members, those with the highest status". D. Martin, "Tongues of Angels and Other Status Indicators" *JAAR* 59 (1991), 547–89 at 567.

53. Horrell, *Social Ethos of the Corinthian Correspondence*, 181.

54. Moltmann, *The Spirit of Life* (Section on Charismata); cf. also J. Moltmann, "The Knowing of the Other and the Community of the Different" in *God for a Secular Society* (Eng. trans., London: SCM, 1999), 135–52. See Thiselton, *First Epistle to the Corinthians*, 1009.

55. Thiselton, *First Epistle to the Corinthians*, 1009.

the world rejects them! . . . They simply bear the suffering which comes their way as they try to follow Jesus Christ and bear it for *his* sake. The meek . . . renounce every right of their own and live for the sake of Jesus Christ. When reproached, they hold their peace; when treated with violence they endure it patiently; when men drive them from their presence, they yield their ground. They will not go to law to defend their rights . . . They are determined to leave their rights to God alone . . . Their right is in the will of their God.[56]

Moltmann puts it this way:

"To know God means to suffer God" says a wise old Greek saying drawn from experience . . . This kind of knowledge of God has received its concentrated theological form in the theology of cross, which says that God is hidden beneath cross and suffering, so that the true misery of men and women, which seems to be so God-forsaken is the place where God encounters us.[57]

The necessary and essential members of the church are constituted by the less honourable and unpresentable parts.

Mutual Concern for One Another

In 1 Corinthians 12:24, Paul repeats the argument which he has already put forward in verse eighteen, that God has arranged (*sunekerasen*)[58] the members in the body according to his will and his purpose in joining the body together so that there will be no division within the body (12:25) (*hina mē ē schisma en tō sōmatin*). This seems to echo Paul's purpose in writing his first letter to the Corinthians (provided in 1 Cor 1:10), where the plural term divisions (*schismata* pl)is used. The opposite of schism is to show care for one another. Thus, Collins comments, "Paul's strategic use of the term is an indication of the careful rhetorical composition of his letter."[59] The conjunctions that (*hina*)

---

56. D. Bonhoeffer, *The Cost of Discipleship* (London: SCM, 1959, (2001), 61–63. See Bonhoeffer's comments on Matt 5:3–10. Emphasis original.

57. Moltmann, *God for a Secular Society*, 148.

58. *Sunekerasen* is first aorist indicative of *sugkerannumi*. For the meaning "compose the body (by unifying the members so as to form one organism)," see BDAG, 952.

59. Collins, *1 Corinthians*, 465. Collins notes that the term *schism* in the sense of rupture is rarely found in the literature of the time, except in a document pertaining to the guild of Zeus Hypsistos in an injunction against religious factions.

and but (*alla*) (v. 25) express the alternative by avoiding the rupture of the body. In other words, the ultimate aim here is that members should mutually care for one another: (*to auto huper allelon merimnosin ta mele*) this could be translated as "the same care for one another" (NRSV, RSV); "the same concern for one another" (REB); "equally concerned for all the others" (JB, RV). It is likely to denote the mutual care among one another (the members of the body), "who mutually need each other to function as a body."[60] The care and concern for a person or a group is not aimed at the benefit of the respective person or group, rather at the total care of the whole body. It is likely that Paul has in mind the care and concern that spouses need to have for one another since Paul used the same verb (*merimnaō*) in 1 Corinthians 7:32–34, which denotes care that "absorbs the attention."[61] God has formed the body and has joined its parts in such a way that "the least" members have more honour (12:26–27). The practical implication of the body being joined together and thus having mutual concern for one another is to suffer with those who are suffering and to rejoice with those who rejoice (12:26). In other words, if one member of the body suffers, then suffering could be a common concept in the body politic (compare 2 Cor 11:29). One can imagine that if one part of the body aches, the whole body suffers the same stress and pain. "The mutual experience of suffering represents a Pauline emphasis as does the mutual experience of rejoicing (compare Rom 12:15)."[62]

Individual Members of the Body of Christ (12:27)

The core of Paul's thesis about the body metaphor is reached in 1 Corinthians 12:27, "now you are (the) body of Christ and individually members of it" (*humeis de este sōma Christou kai melē ek merous*). There is no definite article accompanying the word "body" in the Greek text. Hence, Kim suggests, "It is an urgent business of 'now' (*de*) in v. 27 that shifts the mood dramatically from body analogy (12:12–26) to an exhortation for the community (12:27).

---

60. Fee, *First Epistle to the Corinthians*, 615.

61. Thiselton, *First Epistle to the Corinthians*, 1011. Garland suggests, "marriage means committing oneself in a special way to the existence of another by involving oneself with the spouse in a relationship of care and concern, and, given the Lord's teaching about divorce, it is an irrevocable commitment." Garland, *1 Corinthians*, 333. But Fee suggests the contrast between "schism" and "same care for one another" is appropriate in the context of 1 Corinthians 11:17–34, where the division leads to less caring for others. See Fee, *First Epistle to the Corinthians*, 615.

62. Collins, *1 Corinthians*, 465–66.

Now the Corinthian community should live the 'body of Christ' in their social, community life."[63]

I would suggest that the conjuction *de* denotes a shift of mood as well as an emphasis in Paul's purpose for the body analogy in representing relational character. Fee comments,

> Paul is not trying to say something about their relationship to other churches, but about their relationship to Christ and to one another. Thus, he does not mean *the* body, as if they were the whole, nor does he mean a body, as if they were one among many (true as that might otherwise be). Rather, he means something like "Your relationship to Christ (vv. 12–13) is that of being his body."[64]

Paul describes God as the planner and creator of the body and as intending among the believers' mutual concern for one another. Each believer is related to Christ and to one another as a part (*ek merous*) of the body. Each part has its own function to contribute to the body's well-being.

Different Functions in the Body of Christ

Here, Paul explains the differing functions of the body and providing what seems to be a ranking of functions or gifts. The relative pronoun "whom" refers back to members (*melē*, in plural); the whole message about the body is aimed at the "members." "God has arranged" (*etheto*) is repeated as in 12:18 (compare 12:24). First Corinthians 12:27–28 is the only instance in the New Testament where the gifts are listed in hierarchical order. Four of the eight gifts appearing in the immediately prior list (1 Cor 12:8–10) are the gifts of prophecy, powers,

---

63. Kim, *Christ's Body*, 85. Paul exhorts the Corinthian community to get rid of their spiritual hegemony and work towards achieving a loving community (1 Cor 12:31–13:13). A community finds no meaning in itself without love.

64. Fee, *First Epistle to the Corinthians*, 617. Emphasis original. In the statement, "you are (the) body of Christ," the pronoun "you" takes the emphatic position. Barrett writes: "the genitive Xristou (*Christou*) is not of identity but of possession and authority; not, the body, which is Christ, of which Christ consists, but the body that belongs to Christ . . . " Barrett, *First Epistle to the Corinthians*, 292. Also, Yorke suggests, "Paul nowhere makes mention of Christ's personal body; not in v. 13 and certainly not in vv. 14–26 either. In fact, his σῶμα (*soma*) language in vv. 14–26 is completely devoid of Christological content and this is rather strange, to say the least, if Paul were really on his way to announcing metaphorically or mystically the Corinthians are the personal body of Christ Himself (v. 27)." Paul thus summarizes in verse twenty-seven what he wants to say analogically about the Corinthians on the basis of verses fourteen to twenty-six. Yorke, *The Church as the Body of Christ*, 48.

healing, and tongues. Does the ordering also suggest a ranking of gifts? What do we conclude about Paul and hierarchy?

The body politic in 1 Corinthians 12 demonstrates the relations between one another; the body is a system of mutual interdependence and the members of the body act in unity with each other. In the context of spiritual gifts, each member is entrusted to use their gift for the common good, motivated by the greater gift (love) that seeks the welfare of others, and does not seek its own interest. Do the unity and mutual interdependence envisage egalitarian notions? It could be taken as egalitarian, but the idea is rather of a reversal of status – the lower the status, the higher the honour. In another sense, it could mean one person taking the position of the other so that the latter is given the honour of the former and vice versa. It seems to be paradoxical because the less honourable are invested with honour and are the necessary parts of the body.

The instruction to honour the weak looks like an attempt to equalise inequality, but the listing of gifts as first, second, third, etc. seems to suggest a hierarchical order. Rather than dismissing or explaining away either of these features, we need to explain them both, and that is best done not by saying Paul is looking for an absolute or static egalitarianism, nor by saying he allows or advocates for a static hierarchy. Rather, he suggests that whatever hierarchies there are in the body are not to be reinforced but continually compensated for and overturned, by the attention to the least honourable, etc. Whoever finds themselves "on top" at any one time has to keep looking for the needs of the apparently least necessary, and once the lesser member becomes "on top," they presumably have to do the same. This creates a continually revised and continually challenged hierarchy; in other words, a dynamic process which never lets anyone settle down in a position of dominance or "natural" superiority. The people with disabilities are part of the body of Christ and mutual concern and mutual love entail the whole portrayal of the metaphor. There is no question of status or position relating to those who are able-bodied or not; rather, the love of Christ joins all together as the one body of Christ and at the same time individual members of it. Mutual building-up and mutual care runs throughout all for the well-being of the body.

Love that Encompasses Weakness (1 Cor 13)

I would like to quote the words of Catherine Wybourne,

> Love is more easily experienced than defined. As a theological virtue, by which we love God above all things and our neighbours as ourselves for their sake, it seems remote until we encounter it

enfleshed, so to say, in the life of another – in acts of kindness, generosity and self-sacrifice. Love is the one thing that can never hurt anyone, although it may cost dearly. The paradox of love is that it is supremely free yet attaches us with bonds stronger than death. It cannot be bought or sold; there is nothing it cannot face; love is life's greatest blessing.[65]

It is true that love is more of giving rather than receiving. I found the world's most sincere love in the life of children with special needs. Some of them may find it very hard to express in words (they cannot speak); for some it is difficult to express by touch (their limbs are affected); some find it hard to express through their eyes (because they are blind); some find it difficult to express through a hug (they cannot reach us and walk or run towards us); some cannot even communicate through facial expressions, emotions, or body (because they are severely intellectually disabled); yet they know, sense, feel, smell, and hear love expressed in its own language of sincerity. This lesson is being taught by the children with special needs at Deepti Special School and Rehabilitation Centre. Their smile communicates its own meaning, and the right meaning can be understood by anyone who is humane. Love reaches its zenith when we spend time with those who are less abled or differently abled. We realise that there are so many people (of all ages) longing for the reciprocal smile, touch, word, or presence, while many who could offer these are running, working, and living with a "so busy and no time" policy.

Paul considers love as an essential ingredient in the Christian life that should guide all actions (1 Cor 13; Rom 12 and 13); thus, the gifts and charismata are irrelevant without it. The pericope in Romans 12:9–21 seems to be similar to the love hymn in 1 Corinthians 13, both preceded by the exposition on the body metaphor, portraying the different dimensions and implications of love in the everyday life of a Christian. Paul develops his ethic of mutuality from the fundamental idea of mutual interdependence in the body politic to "the body in Christ," where relationship is based on genuine love towards one another. It points to the "being in Christ," the belonging and togetherness of the Christian community that hold together people of different status, gender, and ethnic origin around one axis. As Barclay suggests in the context of Paul and multiculturalism:

---

65. http://www.theguardian.com/commentisfree/2012/dec/13/what-is-love-five-theories accessed on 24 August 2015. "What is love? Five theories on the greatest emotion of all," Jim Al-Khalili, Philippa Perry, Julian Baggini, Jojo Moyes and Catherine Wybourne.

> The foundation of Paul's gospel and the basis of its relativization of all cultures is his radical appreciation of the grace of God which humbles human pride and subverts the theological and cultural edifices which flesh constructs. . . . The church exists not for its own sake but to bear witness to the grace of God.[66]

The Christian experience is an apparent expression of the grace of God received. It is not only an individual experience but has social and ethical aspects which are derived from the incorporation into the body of Christ. The grace we receive from God is not something to be kept as one's own possession but something to be passed on to others.

The Place of the Person with Disability in Resurrection

The role of grace can also be seen in 1 Corinthians 15. Throughout the epistle, divine initiative and divine promise are underlying concepts. Verse thirty-five raises the major questions of this section: 1) How are the dead raised? 2) With what kind of body will they be resurrected? Jewish apocalyptic literature puts forward a view that the resurrected body is an organism composed of particles reassembled from those of the rotting or rotted corpse. "The earth shall then assuredly restore the dead [which it now receives in order to preserve them]. It shall make no change in their form but, as it has received, so it will restore them (2 Baruch 49:2; 50:1–2)."[67]

Prior to 2 Baruch, the Pharisees believed in the existence of a transformed form of the body in resurrection; however, 2 Baruch is of the view that "the earth preserves the body intact, as committed to it."[68] The questions in 2 Baruch 49:2 are closely similar to those of 1 Corinthians 15:35; but, while 2 Baruch stresses no change, Paul in 1 Corinthians 15:51 and 15:37a emphasises change in the resurrected body, "we shall all be changed" and "what you saw is not the body that shall be."[69] Paul uses the metaphor of "sowing in the ground to

---

66. J. M. G. Barclay, "Neither Jew nor Greek: Multiculturalism and The New Perspective on Paul," in *Ethnicity and the Bible*, ed. by M. G. Brett (Leiden: Brill, 1996), 197–214, at 213.

67. Translation by R. H. Charles, *Apocrypha and Pseudepigrapha of the OT, II: Pseudepigrapha* (2 vols., Oxford: Clarendon, 1913), 2:508.

68. Charles, *Pseudepigrapha*, 508.

69. Thiselton notes that the Jewish thought in the first century varied in regard to the belief of a resurrection. Maccabees chapter four (cf. 7:3; 9:22; 13:17; 14:5–6; 17:12, 18, 19) replaces resurrection with a more Hellenized view of immortality beginning at the moment of death. Psalms of Solomon speaks of "rising to eternal life" (3:13); but, without elaboration, Josephus distinguishes: immortality of the soul among Essenes; resurrection of the body among Pharisees; and an unbelief in post mortal existence among the Sadducees (*Jewish Wars* 2:8:11, 14; *Antiqui-*

underlie the universal connection between being brought to life as crop or fruit and transformation of form or different mode of existence on continuity of identity."[70] Moreover, in 15:36 Paul stresses "the fact of transformation through death and revivification" and not the necessity of death.[71]

Paul connects the bare grain of the old creation and the body of the new creation (v. 38) and, as Kennedy suggests, states that this miracle of the resurrection is only possible through "the sovereign power of God."[72] In other words, the body is given by God according to his purpose and according to the role he assigned to each creature. This is also parallel to the way in which God apportions spiritual gifts to believers in the body of Christ (12:18). Thiselton suggests:

> Differentiation in accordance with God's sovereign decree in relation to his future purposes remains a fundamental principle of the *"ordering"* (15:24–28; 14:40; 12:4–11), whether of the old creation or the new . . . contrast differentiation and variety which simultaneously promotes a continuity of identity. . . . genuine differentiation and variety reflects the will of God . . . the loss of the very identity which preserves the *otherness of the other as other* and not a mere replication or projection of "the strong" within any group.[73]

Here is an implication for the person with disability. God is the one who designs the body and differentiation, variety, and identity are part of it. "The issue is if no human mind can predict or conceive the shape or form of the as-yet-unseen *soma* (body) of the resurrection, as long as all of this lies in the hands of God the giver who has his own sovereign purposes, the matter is firmly in hand."[74]

Sarx *and Body*

Sarx has different meanings in Paul's epistles. This term is usually translated into English as "flesh." It does not primarily denote the physical and material in contrast to the spiritual, although it is used here with the sense of "the

---

ties 18:1:3–5; cf. Mark 12:18–23). Collins refers to the speculations of later rabbinic literature: cf. e.g. b. Ketubot 11a; b. Sanhedrin 90b; et.al. (Collins, *1 Corinthians*, 563). See also Thiselton, *First Epistle to the Corinthians*, 1263.

70. Thiselton, *First Epistle to the Corinthians*, 1263. The same model is used by Jesus (John 12:24).

71. Barrett, *First Epistle to the Corinthians*, 370.

72. H. A. A. Kennedy, *St. Paul's Conceptions of the Last Things* (London: Paternoster, 1904), 243.

73. Thiselton, *First Epistle to the Corinthians*, 1265. Italics original.

74. Thiselton, *First Epistle to the Corinthians*, 1265, 1266.

material that covers the bones of a human or animal body." Nevertheless, the word "flesh" has a wider semantic range in Greek. Paul uses this term with a meaning similar to the Hebrew word *basar*, which denotes humanity in its creatureliness and vulnerability. Only rarely Paul does use *sarx* to denote afleshy substance common to human people and the animal kingdom.[75] It usually refers to "the whole person, considered from the point of view of his eternal, physical existence. Thus Galatians 4:13 ("infirmity in the flesh") and 1 Corinthians 12:7 (a thorn in the flesh) . . . refer generally to the physical distress."[76] The LXX translation of the Hebrew *basar* has a sense that contrasts strongly with what is strong and transcendent. "The range of meaning extends from the substance flesh (both human and animal), to the human body, to the entire person, and to all human kind."[77] In Romans 8:7–8, Paul uses *sarx* with an ethical meaning denoting "trust in oneself as being able to procure life by the use of the earthly and through one's own strength and accomplishment."[78] Galatians 5:19–20 shows the works of the flesh that are not restricted to the physical or the sensual. As Thiselton argues,

> Flesh in Paul does not denote any "one general thing," it serves as a "polymorphous concept," that is, its meaning is always heavily context-dependent and variable. Hence Paul's exposition of the varied context-dependent meanings even of flesh as substance (both human and animal, v. 39) paves the way admirably for his forceful argument that **body** (σῶμα) also depends on contextual and purposive factors for its meaning (v. 40).[79]

To sum up, the meaning of *sarx* and *sōma* may vary according to the context in which they are used. Here in verse thirty-seven the main thrust is

---

75. Thiselton, *First Epistle to the Corinthians*, 1266. He uses κρέας (*kreas*) to denote animal meat (Rom 14:21; 1 Cor 8:13).

76. J. A. T. Robinson, *The Body: A Study in Pauline Theology*, Studies in Biblical Theology 5 (London: SCM, 1952), 17–18, 19; cf. R. Jewett, *Paul's Anthropological Terms* (Leiden: Brill, 1971), 49–166 and 453–56; W. Bauer, W. F. Arndt, F. W. Gingrich and F. W. Danker, *Greek–English Lexicon of the New Testament and Other Early Christian Literature*, 3rd ed. (London: University of Chicago, 2000), 743.

77. Sand, σάρξ, EDNT, ed. H. Balz and G. Schneider, 3 vols. (Grand Rapids: Eerdmans, 1990–93), 3:230. Cf. flesh and blood in 15:30.

78. R. Bultmann, *Theology of the New Testament* (Waco: Baylor, 2007), 1:239. Cf. 1 Cor 1:29; Phil 3:3–7; Gal 6:13, 14; Jewett, *Paul's Anthropological Terms*, 95–103.

79. Thiselton, *First Epistle to the Corinthians*, 1267; A. C. Thiselton, *Two Horizons: New Testament Hermeneutics and Philosophical Description with special reference to Heidegger, Bultmann, Gadamer, Wittgenstein* (Exeter: Paternoster, 2005), 408–11; See A. C. Thiselton, "The meaning of σάρξ in 1 Cor 5:5," SJT 26 (1973): 204–28. Emphasis original.

"the body that rots in the grave is not the body of the future resurrection." It has been already discussed above that the diversity of the fleshy substances and the bodies in the created order are given by the creator God. "Can it, then, be doubted that the raised body, too, will be different in kind and in nature or 'substance' from the body that has died, according to its new sphere and purpose?"[80] In light of verse thirty-five, Paul states that the resurrection of the dead is ontologically possible.

The discussion shifts from flesh (*sarx*, v. 39) to body (*sōma*, v. 40) with the inclusion of the terms "glory" and "super-earthly." While flesh shows the diversity of the "stuff" of creation, body points to the diversities of "form and character."[81] Diversity is affirmed within creation and transformation.

The bodies are differentiated into heavenly bodies and earthly bodies. Paul sets before his readers "the conceivability, on the basis of a theology of God as creator of diverse orders of being, of a 'sort of body . . . entirely outside our present experience.'"[82] The glory of the heavenly bodies and earthly bodies are also different. *Doxa* (glory or splendour) is heavily used in Paul and also in the rest of the NT; its equivalent in Hebrew is *kabod*, which means weight or weightiness or something impressive. In 1 Corinthians 3:21 and 1 Corinthians 1:31, Paul urges the readers to find their source of elation in Christ, and not in human leaders. As Thiselton affirms, "For Paul what makes even God weighty, impressive, a transcendent source of delight and splendour, is not simply his sheer majestic radiance or luminosity but the light which is the knowledge of the glory of God in the face of Jesus Christ, that is, in his self-giving grace."[83] Therefore, the glory here means God's self-giving manifested in his gracious love in and through Christ.

Diversity also comes to force in verse forty-one. The glory and splendour of the sun, the moon, and the stars are different. They are arrayed in a different order and with different functions in God's arrangement of creation. This corresponds to the "each in its own order" in verse twenty-three and also in

---

80. Thiselton, *First Epistle to the Corinthians*, 1267.

81. Conzelmann, *1 Corinthians*, 282. Church fathers interpreted this verse differently. Calvin suggested the diversity in any sort is foreshadowing the resurrection mode. Calvin, *First Epistle*, 336; Chrysostom, Theodore, Ambrosiaster, and Augustine implied distinction as distinction in honour even between individual believers at the resurrection, which is something beyond the meaning in this verse. Chrysostom, *1 CorHom*, 41:43. Tertullian stresses on God as the creator and diversity within creation and transformation. Ernest Evans (ed. and trans.), *Tertullian: Against Marcion* 5 (Oxford: Oxford University, 1972), 5:10.

82. R. B. Hays, *First Corinthians*, Interpretation (Louisville: Westminster/John Knox, 1997), 271.

83. Thiselton, *First Epistle to the Corinthians*, 1270.

response to God's ordering (or subjecting) (vv. 27–28) of the hierarchy of all beings. The stars are not interchangeable; they each have their own radiance and place or order, and they differ from one another in the way God requires of them. The verb *diapherei* denotes "the inexhaustible wisdom of God to promote differentiation within his coherent purposes" (cf. 1 Cor 12–14).[84]

Discontinuity between the Old Body and the Raised Body

The four aspects of resurrection in verses thirty-seven through forty-one indicate: the discontinuity between the old body (v. 38) and the raised body (v. 42); the power of God to create and enact transformation (v. 38); the variety of modes of existence that lie within the sovereign capacity of God to create; and the continuity of identity suggested in verse thirty-eight as "each . . . its own body."[85] The discontinuity is marked by binaries: perishable/imperishable; dishonour/glory; weakness/power; natural body/spiritual body (vv. 42–44). The first discontinuity is *en phthora . . . en aphtharsia*. The different renderings are perishable . . . imperishable (NRSV, REB, NIV, NJB); in corruption . . . in incorruption (AV/KJV); in mortality . . . in immortality (Collins). The word *phthora* denotes "decreasing capacities and increasing weaknesses, issuing in exhaustion and stagnation," i.e. in a state of decay.[86] In the LXX, these Greek words seem to refer to two Hebrew words: *shachat* and *chebel*. *Shachat* and its cognates mean destruction or termination and also mutilation. The semantic contrast of such decay will be perfection and certainly fullness of life. *Chebel* means *vapour* or breath and also vanity, emptiness, fruitlessness; the semantic contrast lies with the purposive progression of dynamic life-processes, in which satisfaction or delight is based on what is substantial and solid.[87] The state of the old body is corruption, but the raised body is not merely incorruptible or imperishable but entails the reversal of the decay, that is, a solidity of progressive, purposive flourishing in fullness of life. In this state two significant things can be noted; the body provides the vehicle for communicative flourishing and identity recognition in the public, inter-subjective domain of community and it is raised by and through God in the power of the Holy Spirit, thereby giving

---

84. Thiselton, *First Epistle to the Corinthians*, 1271.

85. Thiselton, *First Epistle to the Corinthians*, 1271.

86. Thiselton, "Eschatology and Holy Spirit in Paul with Special Reference to 1 Cor" (MTh Thesis, University of London, 1964), 229; cf. Rom 8:21.

87. The analysis is done by Thiselton, "Eschatology and Holy Spirit," 250.

the new being the dynamic of the living God. Hence, it has meaning beyond imperishability and immortality.

The *atimia*/*doxa* contrast can possibly be rendered as humiliation contrasted with glory or splendour.[88] Humiliation includes both senses of being in contrast to glory or to splendour: Paul's use of the body of our humiliation indicates a lowly state (Phil 3:21) and the shame–honour contrast which stands in opposition to *doxa* or splendour. Humiliation can include mourning, sorrow, grief and the sinful desires and actions of the old body, being the new body free from it. The splendour (compare 15:40–41) denotes that which is weighty or impressive (Heb. *kabod*). The word, radiance, is useful as it has the meaning of the "joy in meeting a loved one after a long absence, the bride or bridegroom at a 'happy' wedding; the meeting of lovers; and especially the eschatological, face-to-face union of God in Christ and the spirit-filled believer (v. 44)."[89] This state of splendour indicates the end of sin and death (vv. 44, 52, and 54–57) and also transformation into Christ-likeness (vv. 49–57).

The third contrast is between weakness and power. Weakness further develops the topics of decay (v. 42) and humiliation (v. 43a). Weakness denotes decreasing capacities and incapacity to achieve competency and proper effectiveness, but power is the capacity to carry through purposes or actions with proper effectiveness. The pre-resurrection body is "sown in weakness that expresses frailty, fragility, vulnerability, and constraints of human existence without diminishing the power of the cross, which is the pre-supposition for the triumph of the resurrection mode of existence."[90] Power is the reversal of the decay (v. 42), the splendour (v. 43a) which characterises the gifts, activity, and agency of the Holy Spirit (v. 44). In this epistle, power is the capacity to effect and to activate and has also a transformative dimension (2 Cor 5:17).

The fourth contrast is between natural body and physical body. This verse was often interpreted in light of verse fifty where it states that flesh and blood cannot inherit the kingdom of God. Jeremias argued that flesh and blood do not refer to the corrupted corpse, but to the weakness and sinfulness of the

---

88. The Greek noun ἀτιμία (*atimia*) means dishonour, shame, disgrace (W. Bauer, W. F. Arndt, F. W. Gingrich and F. W. Danker, *Greek-English Lexicon of the New Testament, and Other Early Christian Literature*, 3rd ed. [London: University of Chicago, 2000], 120). It is translated as dishonour in NRSV, NIV, and AV/KJV.

89. Thiselton, *First Epistle to the Corinthians*, 1273.

90. Thiselton, *First Epistle to the Corinthians*, 1274.

human nature.[91] Salvific transformation is essential for the dead and the living in order to take part in the kingdom of God.

The Nature of the Resurrected Body

Adam is the representative of the old creation, and the natural body has its character from him (v. 45). The spiritual body is the creation of Christ who is the life-giving spirit (v. 45). The resurrection mode of existence is characterised by the reversal of decay, splendour, power, and being constituted by the Holy Spirit.

> . . . **raised body** as a form or mode of existence of the whole person including every level of inter-subjective communicative experience that guarantees both the continuity of personal identity and an enhanced experience of community which facilitates intimate union with God in Christ and with differentiated "others" who also share this union.[92]

The resurrection body is "purposive" and a "dynamic crescendo of life" that is not caught up in a static ending. Theissen notes that Paul presupposes the existence of a new world.[93] This new world is characterised by love and the raised body gives meaningful experience of receiving and giving creative love. Luther rightly observes, "It is really the work of God . . . it will not be a body that eats, sleeps, and digests, but . . . has life in Him . . . lives solely of and by the Spirit."[94]

The flesh and blood (v. 50, LXX) denote the weakness and vulnerability of humans. The transformation is a movement from weakness to power and also from sin to holiness (v. 50). Here "Paul underlines the necessity of transformation as the prerequisite for inheriting God's active reign in post resurrection realm."[95] In verses fifty-one and fifty-two Paul twice mentions "we will be changed," denoting that resurrection and transformation happen to both the living and the dead and both will share resurrection/transformation. The verb

---

91. J. Jeremias, "Flesh and Blood cannot Inherit the Kingdom of God," NTS 2 (1955–56), 151–59.

92. Thiselton, *First Epistle to the Corinthians*, 1279.

93. G. Theissen, *Psychological Aspects of Pauline Theology*, trans. J. P. Galvin (Edinburgh: T&TClark, 1987), 365, 388.

94. Martin Luther, *Luther's Works*, vol. 28, *Commentaries on 1 Corinthians 7 and 1 Corinthians 15* (St. Louis: Concordia, 1973), 9–214, 187–92.

95. Thiselton, *First Epistle to the Corinthians*, 1292.

allassō means to change or to alter, referring to a change of form that will be instantaneous. The body will be raised without the degenerating decay; rather, it will see the reversal of decay, that is, it will flourish.[96] The resurrection and transformation has become real through the victory of Jesus Christ; the perishable body puts on imperishability and the mortal body puts on immortality through the victory over death, sin, and law. This has not only a future connotation; it is also a present gift of grace to the believers. Therefore, believers share in the victory in their present life but experience its consummation at the end, at the last day. "When God raised Jesus, the benefit was not for him alone: rather, all of us in . . . the body of Christ share in the victory."[97]

In the context of this book, the key question is: What will be the state of the person with disability in the resurrection? The answer is: All will be raised and there will be no more disability once the transformation has occurred. The perishable body has weakness and vulnerability, but the non-perishable body is resurrected and transformed by the victory of Jesus Christ. It is through the grace of the cross that resurrection and transformation happen. Therefore, the person with disability will sing:

> Where, O disability is your victory?
> Where, O disease is your victory?
> We have a transformed body through the victory of Jesus Christ,
> We will give thanks to God in our body,
> We will make visible the life of Jesus in our bodies.

Conclusion

Paul, in contrast to the Corinthians' preoccupation for strength, power, wisdom, and nobility, makes a radical preferential option for the weak, the powerless, and the foolish, highlighting their significant role in God's salvific plan. The weak is inclusive of both physically and intellectually challenged people. What is despised by the world is accepted by God. This indicates the subversion of human values that are defined and nurtured by the rich and powerful. Paul bases his arguments on the *theologiacrucis*: the cross exposes and challenges all dominant notions of power, wisdom, and influence – and shows the world the power of the powerless and wisdom of the foolish. The experience of Christ on the cross has close correspondence with that of people

---

96. Thiselton, *First Epistle to the Corinthians*, 1297.
97. Hays, *1 Corinthians*, 276.

with disability. On the cross, Christ has voluntarily embraced disability and thus stands in solidarity with the experiences of the people with disability. And, by virtue of his resurrection, he imparts hope to the otherwise hopeless situation of the person with disability.

Paul wants to show that the weak, namely, the persons with disability, are indispensable for the well-being of the whole body of Christ. God has equally incorporated both the strong and the weak into the church, the body of Christ. Paul's usage of strong–weak binaries should not be misread in a hierarchical way; they should be read only in a complementarian way. Their interdependence is highlighted in the koinonia of the Spirit in which the weak are not despised according to human norms of status, but are honoured by virtue of being part of the body of Christ. Here, Paul relies on a pneumatological ecclesiology in which each member of the body is a recipient of the gift of the Spirit. Being part of the body of Christ and also recipients of the gifts of the Spirit is a highly redemptive experience for people with disabilities. With their unique gifts, they contribute to the building up of the church.

Paul places great emphasis on a theology of resurrection. He makes a strong case for the resurrection on the basis of the historical truth of the resurrection of Jesus. His defence of the resurrection is intended to be a simultaneous, two-pronged attack: first, on a materialistic view of the existence of life after death and resurrection and, second, on a sort of spiritualised understanding of the resurrection that denies a bodily resurrection. Taking Christ's bodily resurrection as the foundation of the Christian hope; mustering proof from the plant world, the animal world, and astronomy; and using the finest rhetorical skills he has made a very strong, even irrefutable, case for the truth of the resurrection.

The implication of bodily resurrection is of paramount significance for the experience of a person with disability. Primarily, it means their dysfunctional bodily situation should not be despised. Jesus Christ, by retaining the marks of his wounds and sufferings in his glorified body, shows that God does not despise their bodily situation. Additionally, there is scope for the continuation of the identity of the persons with disability, but in the glorified state their affliction will not be disabling any more.[98] Finally, in this analysis of the identity and experience of the weak grace is the common thread that is implicitly always present. We will discuss the significance of grace for the identity and experience of a person with disability in the following chapter.

---

98. Yong, *Bible, Disability and Church*, 135.

5

Comfort in Affliction and Power in Weakness

A Study on 2 Corinthians 1:3–10 and 12:7–10

Introduction

In his first letter to the Corinthians, Paul wrote about his weakness, affliction, and sufferings and the power and comfort he received from God to endure those sufferings. That power and comfort was not only beneficial to himself, but also to others undergoing a similar crisis. The opponents of Paul were self-boasting about their own standards and evaluating Paul according to the standards of their secular environment; Paul, in contrast, gladly boasted in his weaknesses for within weakness he found a source of God's power. This chapter analyzes two significant passages dealing with affliction and a persistent problem (or illness) that Paul had faced in his life (2 Cor 1:3–11 and 2 Cor 12:7–10 respectively), and the comfort, grace and power that sustained him in the midst of crisis and suffering.

Mutuality in Affliction and Comfort

> Blessed be the God and Father of our Lord Jesus Christ, the Father of mercies and the God of all consolation, who consoles us in all our affliction, so that we may be able to console those who are in any affliction with the consolation with which we ourselves are consoled by God. For just as the sufferings of Christ are abundant for us, so also our consolation is abundant through Christ. If we

are being afflicted, it is for your consolation and salvation; if we are being consoled, it is for your consolation, which you experience when you patiently endure the same sufferings that we are also suffering. Our hope for you is unshaken; for we know that as you share in our sufferings, so also you share in our consolation.

We do not want you to be unaware, brothers and sisters, of the affliction we experienced in Asia; for we were so utterly, unbearably crushed that we despaired of life itself. Indeed, we felt that we had received the sentence of death so that we would rely not on ourselves but on God who raises the dead. He who rescued us from so deadly a peril will continue to rescue us; on him we have set our hope that he will rescue us again, as you also join in helping us by your prayers, so that many will give thanks on our behalf for the blessing granted us through the prayers of many. (2 Cor 1:3-11)

Paul usually follows the epistolary salutations in his letters with an expression of thanksgiving for the divine grace. In 2 Corinthians 1:3–11, Paul opens with a thanksgiving to God for the comfort he received from him. The pericope is all about Paul's experience of God's comfort and encouragement in the midst of affliction and sufferings. He explains that the affliction he experienced in Asia made him renounce all hope for survival and that the intervention of God with his comfort in times of affliction rescued him from the death. The term "affliction" is used three times in this passage,[1] "suffering" is used four times,

---

1. Schlier, θλῖψις, *TDNT*, Vol. 3, ed. Gerhard Kittel, trans. and ed. Geoffrey W. Bromiley (Grand Rapids: Eerdmans, 1965), 143–48, at 143. There are numerous references to θλῖψις in the New Testament.

According to the New Testament, affliction is necessary for the Christian life. Paul is also a man who suffers affliction (2 Cor 1:4; 7:4; 1 Thess 3:7; 2 Cor 4:8; 7:5; 2 Cor 1:5; Col 1:24). First, the sufferings and affliction of the church and the apostle are regarded as sufferings of Christ yet to be filled up (Col 1:24; 2 Cor 1:5; Phil 3:10). Second, in 2 Corinthians 4:10, the apostle experiences in his physical existence the death suffered by Jesus Christ. The third characteristic is that there is an eschatological tribulation. The eschatological significance of the tribulation can be seen in 1 Corinthians 7:26. The power common to all afflictions is death at work in it. Paul experiences the death of Jesus Christ in his own body. In other words, afflictions are deaths (2 Cor 1:8; 4:10, 11, 12; 2 Cor 11:23; Rom 8:26). "And it is clear that in this last time the necessary suffering of Christ in His members is an experience of the concrete effects of the power of death which Christ has already broken in His death and resurrection" (cf. Phil 3:10; *TDNT*, 3: 147).The power of death in affliction affects man in his carnal existence (2 Cor 7:5). The apostle fulfils the sufferings of Jesus in his *sarx* (Col 1:24). He bears the marks of the death of Jesus Christ in his body (2 Cor 4:10) and in his total psycho physical constitution (2 Cor 7:5). In affliction death shatters the earthen vessel (2 Cor 4:7) and destroys our outward man and the outwardly oriented and outwardly experienced life with its essential contingency and corruptibility (2 Cor 4:16). Paul overcomes the death operative in him by offering up his life in

and "comfort" ten times; comfort becomes the catch word in this passage. Paul finds himself being a recipient of the divine comfort with the purpose of giving comfort and encouragement to those who are in a similar condition of distress.

Paul's pattern of thought is significant in this passage: God's comfort in Paul's suffering propels him to comfort others who suffer (v. 4); Paul's experience of Christ's suffering is abundant as were the sufferings of Christ (v. 5); Paul's suffering ultimately leads to the comfort of the Corinthians as they patiently endure sufferings (v. 6); finally, as the Corinthians experience suffering, they will also experience God's comfort through Paul (v. 7). In essence, because Paul had experienced disabling situations in which he also experienced God's comfort, he was able to comfort others who go through challenges and suffering due to disability. Likewise, I have seen people with disabilities, who have their own challenges of various kinds, going out of their way to help, comfort and encourage others who are going through challenging situations.

God: Source of All Comfort

The adjective, *eulogētos*, is used to refer to God's blessing[2] while *eucharisteō* (v. 11) is used to express gratitude towards God for his work. Paul acknowledges with much delight the special strength given by God in the midst of trials that overwhelmed him. In v. 3, he twice addresses God the Father, although the order is reversed in the second part of the verse. The divine fatherhood of Jesus is affirmed since "God is not only his 'Father' but also his 'God' . . . One characteristic of divine fatherhood is tender mercy, a gracious and gentle compassion towards his children in their creatureliness and sinfulness."[3] A very important term in this passage is *pasēs paraklēseōs* which means "comfort of every kind."[4] The rendering of this word in the New Testament is always more

---

faith to God who raises the dead. The faith which offers life back to God, and which overcomes the temptation of mortal tribulation is active in patience. For in patience hope is sustained and there is comfort which comes to those who suffer through Christ (2 Cor 1:5f.; Rom 5:3). The patience with which suffering is accepted by faith is fulfilled in the joy brought by the Holy Spirit.

With the acceptance of affliction by faith, there is edification of the community. The word of God becomes a personal promise of comfort to others (2 Cor 1:4f; 4:10f; Col 1:24; Eph 3:13; 1 Thess 1:6f.). Also, Paul speaks about affliction–joy, God of Comfort (1 Cor 7:5–16), and affliction–joy and poverty–wealth (1 Cor 8:2).

2. εὐλογητός is a verbal adjective and its Hebrew equivalent is *baruk* (Aramic *berik*), which means "blessed." It introduces what may be called either a doxology or a eulogy.

3. Murray J. Harris, *The Second Epistle to the Corinthians,* NIGTC (Grand Rapids: Eerdmans, 2013), 142.

4. Harris, *Second Epistle to the Corinthians*, 143. "Ever ready to console" (TCNT), "whose consolation never fails us" (NEB, REB); "who gives every possible encouragement" (NJB); God's

than soothing sympathy. It has the connotation of strengthening, helping, and making strong. The Latin word for comfort is *fortis*, which means "brave."[5] Paul undoubtedly has in mind his devastating affliction in Asia (2 Cor 1:8–10) and his debilitating depression in Troas and Macedonia (2:12–13; 7:5–6).

From the beginning of his Christian life, Paul understood his calling to suffer for the name of Christ (Acts 9:15–16). "Suffering for Christ was ever his destiny as the apostle to the Gentiles (1 Thess 2:2; cf. Col 1:24; Eph 3:13)."[6] The fact that Paul calls God, "Father of all mercies" and "the God of all encouragement," is significant as the former recalls the Jewish prayer, the "Shema." The term *paraklēsis* is the key word in the whole discussion. The root is found ten times in five verses and is also found throughout the epistle. In the background of this passage is an emphasis of comfort, which has a special place in the messianic deliverance of the people of Israel. The different renderings of this term are: comfort (RSV, NIV, Barrett); encouragement, consolation (NEB); and the God who comes to help (TEV/GNB). Here, the apostle highlights his own experience of God's character as someone compassionate and comforting.

Purpose of Affliction as Enabling

In verse four, Paul explains how God encourages/comforts/consoles us in all afflictions and, as a result, we can encourage those in any trial by the same encouragement we ourselves have received from God. *Paraklēsis* is the leading word in verses three to seven. This term has three basic meanings: encouragement/exhortation, appeal/request, and comfort/consolation.[7] In 2 Corinthians, Paul repeatedly refers to comfort as a "consolatory strengthening" that affords spiritual refreshment in the face of adversity. This consolation involves more than mere words of sympathy and verbal consolation – God being the source of it – mediated by fellow believers (7:6–7, 13). The timeless comfort ("who

---

limitless compassion (Ps 145:9; Mic 7:19) and never-failing comfort of every variety (cf. Isa 40:1; 51:3, 12; 66:13).

5. Schmitz, παρακαλέω, *TDNT* 5, ed. Gerhard Friedrich, trans. and ed. Geoffrey W. Bromiley (Grand Rapids: Eerdmans, 1967), 793–99 at 797, 798.

6. R. P. Martin, *2 Corinthians*, WBC 40 (Waco: Word Books, 1986), 142.

7. W. Bauer, W. F. Arndt, F. W. Gingrich and F. W. Danker, *Greek–English Lexicon of the New Testament and Other Early Christian Literature*, 3rd ed. (London: University of Chicago, 2000), 618a, b. See also O. Schmitz and G. Stahlin, παράκλησις, *TDNT* 5, ed. Gerhard Friedrich, trans. and ed. Geoffrey W. Bromiley (Grand Rapids: Eerdmans, 1967), 773–99; J. Thomas, παρακαλέω, *EDNT*, ed. H. Balz and G. Schneider, 3 vols. (Grand Rapids: Eerdmans, 1990–93), 3.23–27; N. Turner, *Christian Words* (Edinburgh: T&TClark, 1981), 73–78.

always comforts") is depicted here and has overtones similar to verse three.[8] The purpose of God is to enable the one who receives comfort in suffering so that they will comfort others.[9]

God's comfort in Paul's affliction and distress enabled him to transmit the same comfort to those who are facing similar situations. His experience is not only beneficial for himself (driving him more to divine care and comfort), but also for his fellow believers. Paul is not communicating that he is the source of comfort, "rather the spiritual principle he is enunciating is that Christians' experience of God's help, consolation, and encouragement in the midst of life's afflictions constantly qualifies and empowers them to communicate the divine 'comfort' to others who face troubles of any variety."[10] Epictetus and Seneca refer to the principle that one's own experience of suffering can aid those who are in the similar situations.[11] Paul applied to his converts the same encouragement he received from God. Paul here acts as a mediator to pass on the comfort to the Corinthians. "Present tense of παρακαλούμεθα highlights the constancy and even the predictability of God's comfort: παρακλήσεως follows θλῖψις as surely as day and night."[12] Affliction is followed by encouragement (the theme of encouragement in affliction is a recurring theme in chapters one through seven). God's comfort is always available; moreover, God is the source of comfort – this is the greater emphasis within these verses.

Abundant Comfort through Christ

Verse five makes clear that, just as Christ's suffering overflows for us, so also his encouragement overflows for us. There are two parallelisms in this verse: *perisseuei ta pathēmata . . . perisseuei . . . ē paraklēsis* and *eis ēmas . . . ēmōn*. Paul presents God as the father of mercy and the God of all comfort. God's comfort reaches us through Christ. Paul views his sufferings as the suffering of Christ and those sufferings equipped him to impart God's comfort to others. "Paul discerned a divinely ordered correspondence between the intensity of

---

8. Timeless affirmations of God can be seen in 2 Corinthians 1:3; 1:4; 1:9; 7:6; 13:11. See for more discussion Murray, *Second Epistle to the Corinthians*, 528.

9. Different translations are: "so that we may be able" (RSV, NRSV), "enables us" (NAB), "so that (we are able)" (NJB).

10. Harris, *Second Epistle to the Corinthians*, 144.

11. Epictetus, *Discourses*, 3.23.8 and Seneca, *Ad Polybium de Consolatione* 15.5. Refer also H. Windisch, *Der ZweiteKorintherbrief* (Göttingen: Vandenhoeck und Ruprecht, 1924), 39.

12. Harris, *Second Epistle to the Corinthians*, 145. παρακαλούμεθα (*parakaloumetha*) παρακλήσεως (*parakleseos*) θλῖψις (*thlipsis*).

his suffering and the adequacy of God's comfort. It was precisely because the divine comfort always matched his apostolic sufferings (v. 5) that Paul was enabled to mediate that comfort to others (v. 4)."[13]

What does the suffering of Christ refer to? It may not be the atoning sacrifice as it is once for all and a completed event (Rom 6:10; Rom 5:8–10). This may be similar to what is found in Colossians 1:24, where Paul affirms that in his own person he is filling up what is lacking with regard to the afflictions of Christ. This verse could be referring to the sufferings associated with Christ, or the sufferings imparted by Christ on his followers (Acts 9:15–16). A person "in Christ" and "for Christ" is sharing the sufferings of Christ. Therefore, Paul says that he shares in Christ's suffering (2 Cor 1:5) and the Corinthians were also part of that suffering (2 Cor 1:7).

These sufferings include both physical, psychological, and spiritual suffering. Paul suffered physically due to the stoning at Lystra (Acts 14:19; cf. Gal 6:17); furthermore, he had daily pressure of anxiety for all the churches (2 Cor 11:28), showing his spiritual sufferings for Christ's sake. The Macedonian ordeal also caused him physical and internal affliction (ἄνεσιν) of the body and internal fears (2 Cor 7:5). Lastly, Paul describes the illness of Epaphroditus, who faced death while serving Christ and "risking his life to complete what was deficient in your service to me" (Phil 2:30). The physical or spiritual sufferings he experienced due to testifying to the gospel and on behalf of Christ can be considered as the sufferings of Christ.

Patient Enduring (2 Cor 1:4–6)

There is a divine purpose behind Paul's suffering. Paul knew that, in affliction, divine encouragement through Christ is received. The purpose of trials is the encouragement and salvation of the Corinthians. In other words, Paul suffers, and the Corinthians are benefiting out of his affliction. This benefit to the Corinthians through Paul's suffering is repeated twice in the verse. The end of Paul's sufferings is the comfort of the Corinthians.

The salvation mentioned in this verse does not mean Paul is to be seen as a saviour figure, but rather as a mediator between Christ and the Corinthians. The salvation further defines the nature of the comfort: it shows the spiritual well-being, a person's attainment of peace, joy, and security in the renewing experience of God's presence. There is also a close resemblance Paul wants to draw here between his sufferings and the sufferings of the Corinthians.

---

13. Harris, *Second Epistle to the Corinthians*, 145.

There are four different stages in the progression of Paul's thought in verses four to six:[14]

   a. Paul's *thlipseis* (vv. 4, 6) or *pathēmata* (v. 5, 6)
   b. God's *paraklēsis* (vv. 3–6) given to Paul through Christ (v. 5)
   c. The Corinthians' *thlipseis* (v. 4) or *pathēmata* (v. 6)
   d. God's *paraklēsis* (vv. 4, 6) given to the Corinthians through Paul (v. 6).

Murray rightly says that "Paul's suffering of affliction and endurance of trial ultimately benefited the Corinthians in that he was thereby equipped to administer divine encouragement to them when they were afflicted and to ensure their preservation and spiritual well-being when they underwent trial (cf. Eph 3:13; 2 Tim 2:10)."[15] Suffering and the divine encouragement given to Paul in weakness is the same theme he refers to in 2 Corinthians 10–13 (where he receives strength in weakness). Furthermore, in 2 Corinthians 4:7–12, Paul explains how they overcome their crisis with the life of Jesus being at work in their mortal body.

Partnership in Suffering (v. 7)

In verse seven Paul says, our hope for you is unshaken; for we know that as you share in our sufferings, so also you share in our consolation. "What unites the apostle's present trials and the carryover of his encouragement into the lives of the people is a 'confidence,' the confidence he cherished that all was well with his readers."[16] There is a divine purpose in Paul's suffering for Christ's sake. The whole passage shows that

> those who receive encouragement from God are qualified to enter sympathetically into the experience of others whose pathway leads them through a vale of tears (vv. 4, 6, 7). Sympathy is love perfected by experience, . . . so Paul the apostle is not a man who lives a detached existence, untroubled by hard knocks in life and by the same token he is no aloof pastor, remote from the people whom he ministers . . . he who has experienced one kind of afflic-

---

14. Harris, *Second Epistle to the Corinthians*, 147, 146.
15. Harris, *Second Epistle to the Corinthians*, 149.
16. Martin, *2 Corinthians*, 40.

tion is particularly qualified to console others in the same and all circumstances.[17]

Example of Paul's Suffering and Deliverance (vv. 8–11)

In verse eight, Paul describes one of the incidents in which he was affected with affliction and how he received God's comfort in this. In Asia, Paul and his friends were excessively weighed down, beyond their strength, and they despaired even for survival, "The burden was beyond measure and beyond ability to endure, we were utterly crushed." The verse also possibly implies that Paul's affliction in 2 Corinthians 1:8–11 was a painful life-threatening illness. He had given up the hope of survival and received a verdict of death. The affliction made him rely completely on God, and refrain from self-dependence and dependence on his own resources. He passed through the stage of putting confidence in himself and his powers to the stage where he could only trust in God. "He had learned the spiritual lesson that for the Christian self-reliance not only is inadequate to meet the demands of a life that is pleasing to the Lord (see 5:9; Col 1:10) but also constitutes an affront to God on whom we are totally dependent for our physical and spiritual well-being."[18] Paul's deliverance from affliction was brought about by God who can raise the dead. God's distinctive feature of raising the dead is mentioned, implying that since God can raise the dead, all the more can he rescue the dying from the grip of death (Rom 4:19). Paul proclaims about the delivering hands of God and puts his hope in him that "he will continue to deliver us."

Verse eleven shows how the Corinthians supported Paul in his affliction through prayers. Divine deliverance can be received through the intercessory prayer of others (Phil 1:19; Phlm 22). Here, Paul's appreciation of the prayers of others and his request to the Corinthians that they also pray for him show interdependence or mutual care and concern among the members of the body of Christ (1 Cor 12:25–26). Paul relates deliverance as a blessing or a gift (*charisma*) from God, which is granted through the prayers of many and prompts thanksgiving to God. In other words, the cycle of thought that is evident here is: the Corinthians pray for Paul's deliverance; God delivers Paul; then,the Corinthians thank God for his deliverance. People with disabilities need prayer support, which would either lead them to healing or will sustain and strengthen

---

17. Martin, *2 Corinthians*, 146.
18. Harris, *Second Epistle to the Corinthians*, 157.

them with grace as they continue in their challenging situation. The mutual relationship between Paul and the Corinthians becomes evident in the context of affliction: he requests the Corinthians to continuously support him through prayer, so that God might deliver him in future instances of affliction.

Affliction as an Opportunity

In 2 Corinthians 1:1–10, Paul conveys to the Corinthian church the experience of affliction, and suffering controls the attitude of a person who undergoes affliction. Sufferings or affliction are not received with joy, and human beings long for joy and comfort in this world they live in. Suffering and affliction cause us pain and discomfort. Those undergoing suffering or affliction want to receive sympathy or empathy from others.

Suffering and affliction also affect the emotions of a person. Emotions can often control the attitude of a person and attitude determines the reactions to the situations and surroundings. It is possible to react to situations in either a positive manner or a negative manner; how we respond sends messages to those with whom we speak or interact. Our attitude helps us make decisions in crises and influences whether we respond actively, passively, or not at all. Furthermore, circumstances are unique to each person. In other words, the situation I am facing is not the same situation others are facing. There may be some similarities, but each person has their own struggles, their own "back story" influencing their emotions and attitudes, and, consequently, their own responses to the situations they face.

Another important truth is that humans cannot control their destiny. In such a critical situation, we realise God is the source that controls our destiny and hence we try to rely on that source for strength and complete deliverance. The situations we are caught up with may not be changed by ourselves, but our attitude can be changed and we can control our attitude towards situations.

In this passage, Paul views affliction as an opportunity. Seeing opportunity in every situation is a significant principle. Paul's response to affliction is important as he finds in it opportunities to:

- Receive comfort from God
- Seek to understand others
- Understand the situation of others who struggle with a similar difficulty (that is, he is mirroring [reflecting] his life on others)
- Pass on the same comfort he received from God to others, since this comfort has no ultimate end in himself, but flows out to others

- Identify with the sufferings of Christ (that is, Christ is mirroring [reflecting] in him)
- Understand the will of God in a new way
- Avoid self-reliance
- Put his complete reliance on God.

It is paradoxical to look at afflictions and suffering with a positive mind since people normally seek pleasure, joy, and comforts. But afflictions and sufferings are part and parcel of life, and welcoming afflictions and sufferings with joy needs more strength and power than one usually has. Thus, Paul here receives strength from God; in other words, God is his strength in affliction and sufferings.

Paul did not mention specifically the nature of affliction in verses three to eight; by doing so, he leaves open the stage for whatever affliction one goes through. He mentions the affliction he had in Asia which the Corinthians may have known about. Strictly speaking, he is giving one example of his repertoire of sufferings as an introduction to the main content of Second Corinthians, with chapters twelve and thirteen being the conclusion of the main theme: the comfort he received from God is a transferrable comfort. Paul speaks about the mercies portioned to each one individually (Rom 12:3); however, the gifts each one receives from God are also for the common good of the church, and not for personal benefit. In other words, the comfort Paul received in his affliction was for the benefit of others. Identification with the sufferings of Christ is another important principle Paul sought to communicate in his letter. His afflictions were an opportunity for him to know more deeply the emotions and struggles that Christ faced in his sufferings.

This passage is important to those who are undergoing any type of affliction or suffering. This book is based on an example of suffering and affliction from my personal life, having a child with special needs, and my enabling to pass on the comfort I received. The experience of the struggles caring for and parenting our child was an eye-opener in many ways. Our earlier perspectives may be different from the perspective we have after undergoing affliction. The latter may be different in its outlook, and beneficial to others. The struggles we pass through may give us vision in different ways: we have a new vision of ourselves, of others, and of Christ/God. Affliction enables us to transfer God's comfort to others. This is a mediating role by which we transfer the comfort received in affliction. This makes me wonder whether God has any criteria in choosing people on whom he can pour out his comfort to.

Grace and Power in Weakness (2 Cor 12:7–10)

The apostle Paul was a miracle worker, yet he suffered non-healing – an ongoing disease or disability. In the context where his apostleship is questioned by a group of opponents, Paul boasts of his weakness rather than his revelatory experience (2 Cor 11–12). Furthermore, in 2 Corinthians 12:7–10 Paul explains how weakness is the way to the power of Christ – the power of someone crucified in weakness. This has been referred to as the "most celebrated paradox in the New Testament."[19] In other words, Paul feels that he is different from his opponents due to his weakness, and he finds his identity in that weakness (2 Cor 12:9).

Boasting of his weakness exalts Christ in himself while boasting of his revelations and visions only exalts himself. Paul in these passages compares himself with his opponents or superlative apostles: they spoke about their revelations that "over-uplifted" or exalted them, while the unidentified thorn or stake[20] made Paul realise his weakness and thus avoid boasting. Although he wished the thorn or stake to be removed as everybody would wish, God's answer included a promise of sufficient grace and perfecting power in weakness. Here one can find the paradox of healing and non-healing in his life. In the end, Paul decided to boast of his weakness, which was profitable since Christ's power rested upon him; in other words, when he was weak, then he was strong.

The Purpose of the Thorn in the Flesh

In this section, we deal with the Pauline perspective of the paradox of healing and non-healing, specifically the issue of the "thorn in the flesh":

> . . . even considering the exceptional character of the revelations. Therefore, to keep me from being too elated, a thorn was given me in the flesh, a messenger of Satan to torment me, to keep me from being too elated. Three times I appealed to the Lord about this, that it would leave me, but he said to me, "My grace is sufficient for you, for power is made perfect in weakness." So, I will boast all the more gladly of my weaknesses, so that the power of Christ

---

19. E. Fuchs, "La faiblesse, gloire de l'apostolat selon Paul. Étude sur 2 Corinthiens 10–13," ("Weakness, glory of the apostolate according to Paul Study on 2 Cor 10–13") *ETR* 5 (1980): 231–53. Cited by R. P. Martin, *2 Corinthians,* 2nd ed. *WBC* 40 (Grand Rapids: Zondervan, 2014), 584.

20. Paul Barnett, *The Second Epistle to the Corinthians*, NICNT (Grand Rapids: Eerdmans, 1997), 567.

may dwell in me. Therefore I am content with weaknesses, insults, hardships, persecutions, and calamities for the sake of Christ; for whenever I am weak, then I am strong. (2 Cor 12:7–10 NRSV)

The complexity of verse seven lies in the paradoxical statements: there is a positive aspect in receiving revelations, but its impact on Paul is negative. As a consequence of receiving great revelations, he was given a thorn in the flesh, a messenger of Satan. The purpose of this was to torment Paul in order to avoid him from being conceited. The word *hina*, here meaning "in order to," twice in one verse, points to three purpose clauses: The reason for giving of the thorn, and that the reason that he should not be proud; the satanic messenger came in order to batter him; this encounter was again to prevent his conceit.[21]

The verse is purposive and intentional (the use of *hina . . . mē*). Paul realises that God's will for him is that he does not become "over-uplifted." Paul speaks of an abundance of revelations (cf. v. 1), in comparison with the claims of his opponents, by giving an example from his life of revelation received fourteen years before (v. 2). The verb *hyperairomai* (too elated) is used in the context of a polemic against his opponents who boasted about themselves and super-inflated themselves.[22] The identical purpose clause *hina . . . mēhuperairomai* ("in order that I should not be too elated") is used twice both at the beginning and at the end of the verse, stressing the weakness of Paul.

God-Given Thorn

In the present passage, Paul explicates how and why the *skolops* (thorn) was given to him by God, namely, a messenger of Satan to buffet him in order to prevent him from being too elated. "The *skolops* was given (a completed action- aorist tense) in order that, a messenger of Satan, might continue to buffet (present tense) Paul, lest he continue to be 'too elated' (present tense)."[23] Why is *skolops* a gift to his life? What difference has it made in his life? Both Paul and his opponents speak of visions and revelations from the Lord, however, unlike them, Paul has not remained over-uplifted. In other words, God has given him a *skolops* to keep on buffeting him so that he will be in the place where God wants him to be. *Skolops* is God's gift as it rewarded him with a

---

21. Martin, *2 Corinthians*, WBC, 606.
22. Barnett, *2 Corinthians*, 568. The word *huperairomai*, which means "to become conceited," to exalt oneself, is found only in one other place in the New Testament (2 Thess 2:4), where Paul speaks about a man of lawlessness as exalting himself against God.
23. Barnett, *2 Corinthians*, 568.

Christ-like character, which involves attributes such as meekness, gentleness, humility, patience, and endurance (2 Cor 10:1; 4:5; 6:4; 12:12).

What is the nature of the *skolops*? Scholars have given their opinions,[24] but there is no consensus or final word regarding the precise meaning of it. *Skolops* was used to refer to both a "stake" and a "thorn."[25] In other words, it meant what is pointed, hence, it refers to an instrument of torture or execution. Moreover, it was used to allude to spikes to impede siege force, having a connotation of violence. In the LXX, *skolops* means only "splinter" or "thorn" (Num 3:5; cf. Ezek 28:24; Hos 2:6). Paul's reference has been thought to be either physical or relational: physical in the sense of an illness, disfigurement, disability, or a moral temptation;[26] or relational, alluding to the opposition against his ministry or the persecution he suffered. The meaning of the term is uncertain, and we can only guess what Paul had in his mind about it. Furthermore, Barnett doubts that even the Corinthians knew the meaning of it.[27] Wilkinson lists the possible meanings of the term in question as follows.[28]

Non-Physical Meanings of Skolops
- Religious Oppression:
    - By an individual
    - By a Jewish or pagan group
- Mental Oppression
    - Exaggeration of a normal state of grief or remorse
    - Neurosis, e.g. anxiety state or hysteria
    - Psychosis, e.g. depression or paranoia

---

24. K. L. Schmidt, κολαφίζω, *TDNT* 3, ed. Gerhard Kittel, trans. and ed. Geoffrey W. Bromiley (Grand Rapids: Eerdmans, 1965), 820–21; P. E. Hughes, *Paul's Epistle to the Corinthians* (NICNT. Grand Rapids: Eerdmans, 1961), 443–46.

25. G. Delling, σκόλοψ, *TDNT* 7, ed. Gerhard Friedrich, trans. and ed. Geoffrey W. Bromiley (Grand Rapids: Eerdmans, 1971), 409–424.

26. See Barnett, *2 Corinthians*, 569.

27. Barnett, *2 Corinthians*, 568.

28. J. Wilkinson, *The Bible and Healing: A Medical and Theological Commentary* (Edinburgh: Handsel; Grand Rapids: Eerdmans, 1998), 205, 206. *Skolops* has certain characteristics: it was given to Paul because of the revelations he received in paradise; it caused him acute pain either physically or psychologically that he requested for its removal; it is a gift of God and a tool of Satan; it involved a permanent condition (implied by the present tense); it was humbling as it prevents spiritual arrogance; it was humiliating, comparable to receiving vicious blows on the face; lastly, it caused weakness in Paul and yet weakness was a source of pleasure and boasting for him. Harris, *Second Epistle to the Corinthians*, 857.

- Spiritual Temptation
  - Pride
  - Doubt
  - Sensuality
  - Ill Temper

Physical Meanings of **Skolops**
- Physical defect
  - Stammering
  - Deafness
- Physical injury
- Organic disease
  - Painful disorder
  - A nervous disease
  - An infection of the eye
  - An infectious disease.

Barnett suggests that the metaphor is relational based on the fact that *skolops* is identified as a messenger of Satan. *Angelos* is generally personal in its use elsewhere by Paul. Furthermore, the verb "buffet" means "to beat with a fist" (Mark 12:65; cf. 1 Pet 2:20). If *skolops* is relational, it might refer to the Corinthian church,[29] the Judaizing anti-Pauline movement, or false apostles and brothers. There are also wide possibilities of personal suffering. The paradox in this verse is that a buffeting *skolops* was given by God and described as a messenger from Satan. The picture here of God permitting this difficulty reflects the life of Job, whom God allowed to be afflicted.

According to Barnett, "This language suggests (1) that Satan was the immediate cause of Paul's difficulty – symbolized by the word *skolops*; (2) that, because the *skolops* was given by God, Satan is subject to God, not his equal (as in dualism); and (3) that in a profoundly mysterious way God was the ultimate source of that *skolops*. Paradoxically, God is the invisible source of this suffering in the life of Paul, his child and minister."[30] Martin suggests, "the thorn was inherently evil and the thorn served a good purpose as a gift from God . . . God is the unseen agent behind the bitter experience."[31] I agree with Harris that some kind of physical ailment most easily accommodates other

---

29. Barnett, *2 Corinthians*, 570.
30. Barnett, *2 Corinthians*, 570.
31. Martin, *2 Corinthians*, 611.

characteristics of *skolops*.³² The thorn serves a good purpose in the life of Paul as a powerful instrument. The thorn can be interpreted in terms of sickness or impairment, since the Greek *asthenian* (12:9–10) clearly refers to physical illness or disease both in the canonical Pauline corpus (Phil 2:27; 1 Tim 5:23; 2 Tim 4:20) and in the Gospels (Luke 9:2; 10:9; 13:11–12). His repeated prayer for its removal also indicates that Paul may have been chronically and permanently afflicted.³³ I think the thorn can involve both physical and relational elements since the physical pain can cause relational problems as well. One can find some examples of this in Scripture: Job was physically afflicted and his friends came to criticize him and find fault with him; also, at the crucifixion of Jesus, he was physically injured and wounded and the people in the crowd directed cruel words to him.

Paul's Prayer

The continuous buffeting of Paul led him pray to the Lord three times for the removal of the thorn, albeit being aware of the spiritual benefit the thorn could bring to him. *Parakaleō* is a common word used in secular Greek for invoking a deity for aid.³⁴ This word is common in the gospels in requests for help or healing (e.g. Matt 8:5; Mark 8:22; Mark 5:17–18). Paul's threefold petition for assistance shows his urgency in removing the thorn. Moreover, the *hina* clause shows the content and not the purpose of the paraklesis: "that it should go away from me," "that it should leave me" (*hina apostē ap' emou*).³⁵

It is explicit in the verse that Paul addressed his prayer for relief from the battering of the angel of Satan to the Lord Jesus. In early church prayers, the prayer was addressed to God the Father (e.g. Phil 1:3; 4:6). Ephesians 2:18 indicates that both Jewish and Gentile Christians enjoy access to the Father through Christ and in one Spirit. But there are instances in which the prayer is addressed to the Lord directly, both by an individual (e.g. Acts 7:59–60; 9:10–17; 22:16, 19; 2 Cor 12:8) and by a group of believers (e.g. Acts 1:24; 9:21; 1 Cor 1:2; 16:22; Rev 22:20). Paul directed his prayer to Jesus because he thinks that the extraordinary revelations that occasioned the giving of the

---

32. Harris, *Second Epistle to the Corinthians*, 858. See also Gordon Fee, *God's Empowering Presence*, 352–53.

33. Yong, *Bible, Disability and the Church*, 87.

34. O. Schmitz, παρακαλέω, *TDNT* 5, ed. Gerhard Friedrich, trans. and ed. Geoffrey W. Bromiley (Grand Rapids: Eerdmans, 1967), 773–99, at 775.

35. Harris, *Second Epistle to the Corinthians*, 860. The possible renderings of this phrase are "to rid me of him" (Weymouth), "to relieve me of it" (Moffatt), or "to take it away from me" (NIV).

skolops (v. 7) come from the Lord (v. 1), who is the healer of illness and also the chief antagonist of Satan and his agents (cf. 1 Cor 15:24; Eph 6:10, 12; Col 2:15).[36]

The frequency of Paul's prayer (three times) stands in an emphatic position before the phrase *ton kurion parakalesa* (I appealed to the Lord). He might have prayed many times, but "many" (*pollakis*) is not used by Paul with *parekalesa* (prayed or appealed). This also reminds us of Christ's threefold prayer at Gethsemane asking the Father that he might take the cup of suffering away from him (Matt 26:44; Mark 14:41). What is the significance of "three times" in Paul's requests? This can mean repeated prayers on one occasion or prayer made at three different occasions, "when a particularly severe attack of the *skolops* prompted an especially fervent request for its removal."[37] This can also be compared to the use of *tris erabdisthēn* in 2 Corinthians 11:25 when Paul speaks about his sufferings: "Three times I was beaten with rods . . . three times I was ship-wrecked." This refers to three separate events with similarity of type.

Enabling and Empowering

The request for the removal of the thorn was denied despite his repeated imploring. However, the answer for the prayer is given in a way that he never expected: Paul received the risen Christ's grace and power to cope with weakness, strictly speaking, the weakness caused by the continuous buffeting of the thorn. This verse is the climax of both 2 Corinthians 12:7–10 and the whole epistle: he was crushed beyond power in Asia (1:8) and as a mere jar of clay he was dependent on "the all-surpassing power of God" (4:7), which is made perfect in weakness (12:9).

Paul's request (v. 8) was in reported speech and Christ's response (v. 9) is given in direct speech. The use of the perfect tense *eirēken* (he said) in verse nine is in contrast with the aorist tense *parekalesa* (I appealed) in verse eight. The petition has been made three times, but now, with an explicit answer received, the act of petitioning to the Lord lies totally in the past and will not be repeated. On the other hand, the Lord's reply, although given only once (after the third petition) was permanently valid. For Paul, his urgent requests were a memory of the past, but God's assuring power was a reality of the present.[38]

While Paul says that what he had heard in paradise is both inexpressible and impermissible, Christ's reply to Paul's prayer was both permissible and

---

36. Harris, *Second Epistle to the Corinthians*, 860.
37. Harris, *Second Epistle to the Corinthians*, 861; Hughes, *2 Corinthians*, 449.
38. Harris, *Second Epistle to the Corinthians*, 861, 862.

expressible. The way of communication is not mentioned, although it was probably through a vision (Acts 18:9), a trance through prayer (Acts 22:17–18, 21), through the testimony of the Spirit (Acts 20:23), or simply through a meditation on the death and resurrection of Jesus Christ that points to the three central concepts in the reply to Paul – grace, weakness, and power.[39] In the Lord's reply to Paul, the two affirmations are significant; the first is a promise and the second is a statement that explains or supports (*gar*) the promise. Harris rightly comments, "Christ assures Paul that the supply of grace (see 13:13) for the carrying out of Paul's ministry, and in particular for the bearing of the pain and buffeting of the *skolops*, would never run dry. He needed nothing more than Christ's grace."[40] In the same vein, in Philippians 4:13, Paul speaks of his self-sufficiency in Christ: "I can do all things through him who strengthens me" (NRSV).

2 Corinthians 12:9a has two parts: the first part and the second part are related by "for" (*gar*) and in the second Christ's power and Paul's weakness are mentioned. Murray understands the terms grace (*charis*) and power (*dunamis*) as synonymous and finds it difficult to identify a precise distinction between these two. Both terms express divine enabling to Paul in order to finish the divine plan. *Teleitai* (made perfect) and *arkei* (sufficient) are both in the present tense, indicating that the enabling is a continuing process and not a one-time event. As the weakness continues in Paul, God's power is also made fully present in him. *Asthenia* (weakness) is not referring to a generic human weakness, but the weakness Paul felt due to the thorn in the flesh.

Scholars have different opinions regarding the nature of the weakness that Paul mentions in v. 10, along with insults, hardships, persecutions, and difficulties.[41] This can refer to the vulnerabilities involved in being a slave of Christ (Rom 1:1): enduring hardships (4:8), being an object of dishonour and scorn (6:8; 1 Cor 4:9–10), being economically poor (6:10; 1 Cor 4:11), and constantly exposed to death (6:9; 11:23; 1 Cor 15:30–31). Harris adds a sense of attitudinal weakness, in other words, the acknowledgement of one's creatureliness and one's impotence to render effective service to God without empowering.[42] The preposition in (*en*) used with weakness shows that in the midst of weakness the power of God is being made perfect, which means that the divine enabling

---

39. Harris, *Second Epistle to the Corinthians*, 862.

40. Harris, *Second Epistle to the Corinthians*, 862.

41. J. Murphy O'Connor, *The Theology of the Second Letter to the Corinthians* (Cambridge: Cambridge University, 1991), 19–20.

42. Harris, *Second Epistle to the Corinthians*, 863.

will be triggered by the acknowledgment of weakness. Furthermore, weakness is a sphere in which God's power is being revealed and is active. This is clear as Paul states that, when he is weak, he experiences the divine power, and this helps him stay strong (v. 10b). The greater the acknowledged weakness, the more evident is Christ's power.[43]

Boasting in Weakness

Therefore, very gladly Paul boasts of his weaknesses, so that the power of Christ may rest upon him. Paul here explains how the power of Christ is at work in him and how this made him realize the power of boasting of his weaknesses. Regarding *astheneia*, the shift from singular to plural is particular to the second part of verse nine, and this can also refer to a particular infirmity or disease. "Very gladly" or "all the more gladly" is used to bring a comparison. Furthermore, Paul would boast of his infirmities rather than complain about them. He finds it weighty and joyful to boast of the weaknesses in his life, rather than praying for their removal and boasting of his revelations through ascent into paradise or his strength.[44]

According to verse nine, the attendance of Christ's presence upon one is significant for both experiencing Christ's power and boasting in weakness; it is a prerequisite "that the power of Christ may come and rest upon me." *Episkēnoō* is a rare word only found here in Biblical Greek, and means to "raise a tent over," "be quartered in,"[45] or to "take up a residence in a tent or dwelling."[46] If the aorist *episkonōsē* is ingressive, it will mean to come in order to rest or take up its abode; if connotative, it will mean to "rest," "dwell," or "reside." Furthermore, some find an allusion to the concept of shekinah, which refers to the glorious presence of God. In the Old Testament, *skenē* represents both the Tent of Meeting and the overshadowing of the divine glory. There is divine enabling and empowering, and also divine protection for Paul as the power of Christ dwells in him. The use of *ē dunamis* is emphatic, that Christ's power may rest upon me. Because of the thorn and its continuous buffeting,

---

43. Black, *Paul Apostle of Weakness*, 159.

44. C. K. Barrett, *A Commentary on the Second Epistle to the Corinthians* (London: A. & C. Black, 1973), 317.

45. H. G. Liddell, R. Scott and H. S. Jones, *A Greek English Lexicon*, 9th edn, with revised supplement (Oxford, 1996), 656s.v.

46. Beyer, ἐπισκηνόω, *TDNT* 2, ed. Gerhard Friedrich, trans. and ed. Geoffrey W. Bromiley (Grand Rapids: Eerdmans, 1971), 599–622.

Paul is all the more experiencing the indwelling of Christ's power and very gladly boasts of his weaknesses.

Pleasure in Weakness

Paul not only boasts in weakness but also takes pleasure in his weakness (v. 10). In this verse Paul explains the reason for taking such pleasure. The divine power working in him is the resurrection power of Christ (Phil 3:10). Paul tries to classify his sufferings in five groups (this seems evident since all the terms in the list are in plural). They are given in Paul's life because of Christ and/or on behalf of Christ.

Christ's Power in Paul's Weakness

"For when I am weak then I am strong" is Paul's personal motto. This is a paradoxical statement that lies at the centre of Paul's life and ministry. This is the attestation of verse nine that "power is made perfect in weakness." "There is an explicit contrast between *dunamis* and *asthenia* and there is an implicit contrast between Christ's power and Paul's weakness . . . When Paul acknowledged his weakness and expressed his dependence on Christ, he became simultaneously powerful with Christ's resurrection power."[47]

Paul lists in verse ten not only his physical illness but also the external afflictions he faced in his service for Christ such as insults, calamities, persecutions, and difficulties. These prompted him to pray for the removal of those weaknesses and affliction. As Harris rightly suggests,

> The Paul who was ταπεινός (10:1) and ἀσθενὴς (10:10) was the true Paul; lowliness and weakness were the hallmarks of his ministry. Yet it was precisely this ἀσθένεια, whether physical, psychological, or spiritual, that caused him to rely wholly on Christ and so occasioned his strength. Behind δυνατός εἰμι we should see an allusion, not to Paul's own ability to cope with the adversity by harnessing all his personal resources, but to his experience of Christ's power, sometimes in delivering him from adversity, sometimes in granting him strength to endure hardship, but always in equipping him for effective service.[48]

Hotan with the subjunctive can rightly be rendered as "whenever"; whenever I am weak, then I am strong (NRSV). "For the moments of weakness are

---

47. Harris, *Second Epistle to the Corinthians*, 867.
48. Harris, *Second Epistle to the Corinthians*, 867, 868.

my moments of my greatest power. If, however, weakness was Paul's conscious attitude of humble dependence on Christ in all circumstance but especially in adverse situations, then correspondingly the experience of having Christ's power resting on him will be a constant reality."[49]

Weakness as an Opportunity

Paul is spiritually mature enough to understand the reason for the sustaining of the thorn in his flesh. The interpretation is possibly intentionally left open as an exhortation to anyone struggling with any sort of thorn in the flesh. Paul's positive response to the thorn is significant as he boasts of it and he gladly suffers it. The thorn can be a physical weakness that is persistently buffeting him. The weakness is the sole criterion by which he receives God's grace sufficiently and also in power. The infilling of power and grace was directly proportional to the weaknesses he suffered. He was weak and whenever he was weak, he was made strong. Outwardly he was weak with all the internal and external pressures and troubles, but inwardly he received power which enabled him and empowered him for his continuous Christian life.

I would like to interpret Paul's letter from a disability perspective as those living with disability are continuing in their problem. Christ's grace and power are exceptionally needed for them to face their crises. His power is needed not only for those who are suffering, but also for those who are taking care of them. God imparts his grace differently according to the particular situation of each person. Thus, one may refer to it as the polyvalence of grace or transmutation of grace. God's grace corresponds with the changing situations of a person's life, involving instances of existential struggles, unceasing pain or discomfort, unexpected challenges, unparalleled adversities, depressing anxieties, sordid uncertainties, and even apparent meaninglessness. The all-sufficient grace can equip us in our struggles; sustain us through pain and discomfort; impart joy when suffering for the sake of the gospel of Christ; embolden us to take on fresh challenges; transform our thinking and open us to opportunities to bless and serve others, even in the adversities; strengthen us to put uncertainty behind us and move forward with the certainty of God's abiding presence; and find meaning even in the moments of apparent meaninglessness.

God has painstakingly taught us the all-sufficiency and polyvalence of grace through our own life with Jyothish. When the doctor said at Jyothish's birth that the chance for the survival of the baby would be very dim, God gave

---

49. Harris, *Second Epistle to the Corinthians*, 868.

us the grace to cling on to his promises. When doctors later diagnosed his disability as cerebral palsy, although we were perplexed at first, God gave us the grace to embark on a new journey in our lives with him. In the moments of unexpected challenges to the health and even life of our son, God gave us a new measure of grace to take on those challenges.

Grace reaches us through a plethora of means: through the reading of Scripture, through prayerful communion with God, by being in the fellowship with fellow believers, and by being lost in worship. And, at times, we receive grace through the visits of guests and their words of encouragement. When, at times, we were drawn to the verges of depression, grace made us lift up our eyes to see the redemptive sufferings of our Lord Jesus Christ and look around us to see children and families suffering without no one to support or impart comfort to them. Thus, a moment of fresh reckoning came to our life – that God's grace does not stop with us. We are not in this world simply in order to accumulate grace upon grace for ourselves: grace must be channelled, it needs to overflow onto others who are desperately in need. God showed us his favour by gifting us a child with special needs in the first place and then enabling us to impart this grace to others who undergo similar situations or even more difficult challenges.

Conclusion

Paul's personal encounter with God in his spiritual journey is made clear in the two passages discussed in this chapter. There is always a personal aspect in any suffering, affliction, and weakness. Only the sufferer knows the intensity of the pain that continuously affects their life. Others can only empathise with or sympathise with the sufferer. Questioning one's own existence in suffering is normal and undergoing suffering is not an easy task. Thus, it is important to have a personal encounter with God in one's own situation.

It is therefore significant for us all that Paul accepted the non-healing aspect in his own life. It is always easy to equate non-healing with unbelief, lack of power in one's spiritual life, or something else that is negative – that causes a "non-response" from God. But Paul's life shows us there can be a new arena of healing in non-healing – through enabling and empowering. The grace and the power of God are as continuous as a person's weakness. It is not given once for all throughout life's suffering, but it is a continuous outpouring according to one's need. In other words, in weakness, one can be made strong.

Paul was fortunate in his life to receive Christ's grace and Christ's power. Through the non-healing and continuous suffering, Paul experienced a direct encounter with God so that divine power was poured into him. It became real when he stated that he wanted to know the power of Christ's resurrection. Thus, this is a costly grace and not a cheap one. Paul paid the price of his own strength, comfort, peace and/or own abilities in order to receive Christ's grace and power in weakness. This offers an important lesson for every human being. There are times when we will be weak or vulnerable, but Paul opens up a new realm of possibility for us in that – to call upon God that we might receive the grace and the power of Christ to overcome.

6

From Brokenness to Blessing

Is the Child with Cerebral Palsy a Gift of God?

This chapter is a narration of my personal story of bringing up a child with special needs, how it has impacted my life, and how my experiences are impacting people who face similar situations.

The First Five Years of Jyothish

Friday 9 May 2008 was the fifth birthday of Jyothish, our fourth child (Jyothish is pronounced "Jow-dhish"; it means "light"). When his friends came to our house with birthday presents and commented, "Jyothish, you're a nice friend," his face was radiant. Seeing his happy face, we and his three loving brothers thanked God. Psalm 127:3 says, "Children are a heritage from the Lord, offspring a reward from him" (NIV). So, can we consider a child born with bad health and chronic illness to be a gift of God? When we look back at the difficult years we have passed through with Jyothish, we often wonder and think about the source of strength we received to face those challenging years – we believe it is nothing less than the grace of God. Jyothish is a precious gift God gave to his parents, who work in full-time Christian ministry.

Jyothish faced so many crises in his life and even in his mother's womb. When the doctor said at the time of his birth, "We have no hope that the child will survive, but we will try to save the mother," Mathew (my husband) was shocked. But he remembered God's promises about Jyothish before his birth, he would be a sign of God's work and that he would be used for God's glory. He began to thank God because he is faithful in fulfilling them. Isaiah 43:2 says,

> When you pass through the waters, I will be with you;
> and through the rivers, they shall not overflow you.

> When you walk through fire, you shall not be burned,
> nor shall the flame scorch you.

These verses assure us that when we face problems, the challenges will not overcome us because we have the assurance of his presence. These promises don't so much seem to promise that we can "defeat" the waters or fire, but rather that they won't destroy us.

Jyothish was born five weeks premature through emergency C-section and he weighed only one and a half kilograms (which is less than three and a half pounds). He had breathing trouble and was in a neo-natal intensive care unit for about eight days. When Jyothish was discharged from the hospital, we gave him special care and attention at home. He began to face difficult situations. His development was delayed and in the eighth month we took him for a check-up. The paediatrician in the Century Hospital, Chengannoor, referred him to the neurologist in the Medical College, Thiruvananthapuram. Under his careful examination in the MRI[1] scan, he was found to have developmental problems. The nerves controlling the motor functions in his left side of the body had not been working at all. It would be quite difficult for him to be a normal child; the doctor expected delayed milestones.

The doctor explained the problems he had seen and his expectations about Jyothish's future. It is usual for a normal child to be able to walk around twelve months of age. However, walking would be delayed in his case. With great care and continued physiotherapy, he could probably walk independently by the time he would be five years of age. My heart was broken; at that very moment I pondered the promises given by God while he was in my womb – "he will be in spiritual leadership like Moses."

We had to travel to different places to give him physiotherapy but Jyothish did not receive any speech or occupational therapy in his first four years, due to the unavailability of such facilities in our locality. Because of the lack of services, we began to experience hardships and agony. It is commonplace to think that a child with disability is a curse or a punishment from God. Moreover, when "loving" ones – relatives, neighbours, friends, even co-believers – began to ask that question it was a blow to us as parents because we were already in the furnace, and we felt like the intensity of the fire had increased. However, we received the prayers, support, encouragement, and love of our parents, siblings, pastors, co-believers, the whole community of Faith Theological Seminary in

---

1. Magnetic Resonance Imaging is a medical imaging technique used in radiology to form pictures of the anatomy and the physiological processes of the body.

Manakala, Kerala (we both teach at the Seminary), and even others who are unknown to us. The days and weeks passed by soaked with tears and enveloped with sighs, waiting for Jyothish to start walking for the first time. At the same time, we began to feel the presence and comfort of God, with the same power which is active in miracle working. When God asked Abraham to sacrifice his only son, he obeyed. But when he climbed the mountain of Moriah, his heart as a father would have been naturally troubled at Isaac's question, "Look, we have fire and wood, but where is the lamb for a burnt offering?" God began to ask me, "Do you know the real pain of Abraham when he was obeying God by sacrificing his son?" I said, "Lord, it is easy to preach that Abraham obeyed, but when it is my experience it is a bit difficult."

Another day, when Jyothish was one year and four months, a servant of God came to our house and said, "It is difficult for a glass to regain the original state if it is broken and is of no use. But if it reaches the hands of its manufacturer, he can mould that into a new shape – into a more useful condition.

Jyothish did not have neck control until he was two years old. He also had chest infections and related problems. In other words, he would be hospitalized regularly. Later, we realised that therapy could help him do better. Thus, we tried to help him at any cost. I thought, "I am the mother of Jyothish and God has entrusted me with the responsibility to help him out in order to have a better life in this world without disability." The prayer continued, we waited upon the Lord and at the same time helped Jyothish with our best efforts.

Another day, God gave me a vision that he would bless Jyothish and help him to be in spiritual leadership like his granddad (his granddad Rev. Dr. T. G. Koshy had been in the Christian ministry for fifty years). I believed that this would happen and began to pray so that this vision would become real. I thought, "Jesus healed people with sicknesses and infirmities; why could that not happen in the case of my son?" Waiting gets tiresome and problematic since a child with sickness affects the various realms and dimensions of a family: social, physical, financial, spiritual, psychological, etc. When Jyothish was one and a half years old (2004), I heard the soft voice of God strengthening me, "Wait, wait, you will see a miracle in your life." God began to lift up our faith gradually. While carrying Jyothish, I was reminded by God of the faith shown by Moses' parents. It is written in Hebrews 11:23 that "by faith" the parents of Moses acted. They hid him for three months and did not fear the command of Pharaoh. God had a plan for Moses, but God wanted his parents also to act in faith. "Faith is the substance of things hoped for, evidence of things not seen" (Heb 11:1). Although I could not see Jyothish as a completely developed normal child, I believed and saw with my inner eyes – the eyes of faith – that he would be made whole. We spoke to him continuously, "Jyothish, whatever be your developmental problems, you will walk independently one day."

We received comfort from God as we were enduring the tensions of having a child with CP. The words and deeds of humans have limitations. In the crucial moments of our life, we really need God's voice, the one who has formed us in our mother's womb, who knows our past, present, and future, and who holds our hand in our journey of life through mountains, valleys, stony soils, thorny, muddy land, scorching heat, and streams of water. There are points in our life when we feel we are alone and that nobody can help us in any way. God is looking forward to the moment when we surrender our lives completely into his hands and say, "Lord, here am I, help me."

Despite our trust in God, patience proved elusive. We watched with a mix of hope and frustration as Jyothish struggled to stand, each attempt ending in a tumble. We were broken and very much depressed about his developmental delay. When my son was nearly two years old, I made a vow: "Lord, I cannot preach until you heal my child." It was difficult for me to proclaim God's goodness while my son remained unhealed.

Nobody heard my conversation with God, but I received a phone call just an hour and a half later inviting me to preach in the Working Women's Conference in the Bible Society, Kottayam. The call was from Evangelist M. C. Kurian; I answered him that it was inconvenient for me to attend this meeting, since I needed to take care of Jyothish. He replied, "This time there is no option; if you tell your experience, surely women attending the conference would be blessed." When we finished talking over the phone, I began to think about Evangelist Kurian, who was also (then) the father of an eleven year old child who is severely affected with CP. I started to empathize deeply with his pain, struggles, and hardships, which led me to become more concerned about other families facing even greater challenges than mine. As a result, I decided to preach at the conference.[2] It turned out to be a profound blessing for everyone and a transformative experience for myself. I came to the realization that even when it feels like no one understands our words or shares our pain, God is there to support us and carry us forward when we feel unable to move ahead.

Before Jyothish was born, we didn't pay much attention to others who might be going through similar situations. Now, we deeply empathize with their pains, struggles, and anxieties. We understand that in India, caring for a child with CP (Cerebral Palsy) can be extremely challenging. Many parents

---

2. I attended this conference as a resource person along with Dr. Joan Chunkapura. See page 108.

are unable to afford the necessary treatment, and some may stop giving timely care due to the financial burden it brings. Once, a friend asked my husband, Mathew, "Is it possible for Jyothish to attend school, maybe in a special school?" Hearing such comments about our disabled child is always painful for us, even though we understand his condition. In response, Mathew quietly resolved to himself, "His first schooling will be in England, not in India."

Meanwhile, I was accepted as a PhD candidate at Durham University, England. I received the news of admission on the same day when Jyothish was diagnosed with CP (when he was nine months old), in India. I began to weigh up both options – taking care of a child with serious developmental problems as his mother or going abroad as a doctoral student. I knew that my child is more precious than my studies.[3] The doctor advised that the mother should be with the child always, since others did not know how to look after such a child and that could lead to complications. I postponed my enrolment for two more years, but God spoke to me, "I will send you to England for studies as well as ministry. When I open ways for you, you should go and should not say 'No.'" I made up my mind to continue teaching ministry in the seminary, as well as my responsibilities of looking after my reward from God, Jyothish, although I was advised by some people to be at home to give full-time care to Jyothish.

After having Jyothish, God began leading us in new pathways. We shared with others the power, love, and the provision of God that strengthen and comfort us to face problems, crisis, and sickness. I thanked God several times after seeing my students recommitting their life to Jesus when I shared my experience. To live a normal life with a child with CP is difficult for the parents. The child needs total time, total attention, and total care. One day I heard my husband praying, "Lord, no matter whether you heal Jyothish or not, we will continue to preach that you are the God of miracles." Then, the amazing day finally came – Jyothish took his first step in walking, two weeks before his third birthday! The whole family thanked God joyfully. Although his left side was weak (he used toe-walking), the joy we had when he made his first step could not be expressed in words. God is faithful in fulfilling his promises.

In the meantime, I received a letter from Durham University checking whether I wanted to begin my doctoral studies that year (in October 2006). I remembered God's word and I obeyed him by responding that I was ready to go, although I was unsure at that time regarding finances, namely, how to cover

---

3. As I was planning to travel abroad for my studies, I was unsure whether my family would join me from the beginning. It needed enough funds and provision for Jyothish's further treatment.

the tuition fee and my living expenses at Durham. Nevertheless, I believed in God's word ("I will work for you"). I got the Durham University scholarship for my first year of studies (2006–2007) and arrived in Durham 27 September 2006, leaving my family back in India. I remember well the day (6 May 2007) when I got an email from the Langham Scholars Director offering me a scholarship[4] for two years 2007–2009. This reminded me of the verse in Scripture that says: "Eye has not seen, nor ear heard, nor have entered into the heart of man, the things which God has prepared for those who love Him" (1 Cor 2:9).

My family reached England the day prior to Jyothish's fourth birthday (8 May 2007). He started his schooling a few months later in September and he was privileged to have loving teachers and caring friends. He had weaknesses, but we believed that God gave us Jyothish as a special gift in our life. God is always watching over people in whom he can reveal his glory and looking to fulfil his plans and purposes in the lives of his children. When we surrender our lives to God's will, he helps us and he will turn the impossible into the possible, for nothing is impossible with God (Luke 1:37). Thus, the following psalm strengthens me in difficult times.

> God is our refuge and strength,
> An ever-present help in trouble,
> therefore, we will not fear, though the earth give way,
> and the mountains fall into the heart of the sea. (Ps 46:1, 2)

Sr. Dr. Joan Chunkapura once preached in a working women's conference on 6 February 2006, "Do not consider the child born with sickness and problems as a curse of God because children are rewards from God. The presence of God and the love of God will be in a special way, with these families that undergo such a crisis." We are wounded in order to comfort others by the comfort of God we received in difficulties. The apostle Paul wrote, "Blessed be the God and the Father of our Lord Jesus Christ, the Father of mercies and the God of all consolation, who consoles us in all our affliction, so that we may be able to console those who are in any affliction with the consolation, with which we ourselves are consoled by God (2 Cor 1:3, 4). We are grateful to God, since he has been preparing and training us for this comforting ministry.

---

4. Langham Scholarship offers financial support for students from the Majority World to study in the UK and Ireland. I received full tution fees and a part of my living expense as a family.

Jyothish's Childhood

Jyothish was privileged to live in Durham, United Kingdom, for three years (2007–2010) when we moved there as a family for my doctoral studies – and where we got to know about the facilities given to a child with special needs in the UK. After an assessment by an educational psychologist, Jyothish was admitted to a mainstream school, St. Hild's School, Gilesgate, Durham. He was very happy with the involvement and participation in school activities and that he was not being side-lined by his peers and teachers.

Jyothish received treatment and therapies regularly following his registration with the NHS; and treatment was continued in all areas of his developmental needs at a child development centre, in Chester-le-Street. A health visitor visited him at home, assessed him, and referred him to different services. He was referred to a consultant paediatrician and then for physiotherapy, occupational therapy, speech therapy, to the orthotics department, and an educational psychologist, all which periodically made assessments and provided treatments. Special furniture and aids, such as a dining chair, corner seats, a commode, a bathing seat, special seating at the school, a laptop to work with etc., were given to him. Jyothish had no pencil control when he joined his school due to the lack of muscle coordination in his hand. He was helped by a staff member continuously for two years and finally he achieved pencil control with his hand. His handwriting was good, being able to write without deviating from the line.

There is a different care scenario regarding service provision and coordination in lower-income countries, where parents have to find the services (and finance) themselves, which are abysmally minimal. A similar centralised scheme in countries like India for the treatment and education by the health and education departments would greatly improve life outcomes for children with disabilities (and their families). After I completed my PhD in 2010 we moved back to Kerala. The nearest school rejected his admission application because of his disability; therefore, he was admitted to a school eight kilometres away from home. It was not the same as the one in the UK. At his school in the UK, he received good support and help. In India, he missed many school days due to sickness. In the UK, the county council takes care of the holistic development of a child. They provide medical help through the NHS and educational help through local schools. Psychologists co-ordinate appointments in the child development centre and make sure to give proper guidance and support on a timely basis. For Jyothish, they provided orthotics, equipments for school and home and therapies are arranged in the school. In India, parents have to find out the medical help and education for their children. There is the absence of proper help at school as well. His left side muscles were weak and tight, and this affected his walking pattern. Daily sessions of lengthy therapy at home instilled in Jyothish a strong aversion towards it.

Four surgeries in five years made him react negatively towards the therapy and treatment. The pain of the surgeries and the follow-up process of being in casts for six weeks after each surgery, rehabilitation therapy afterwards, etc., made him compare his situation with others and question his identity as a physically challenged child. The first surgery done was a tendon release surgery on both legs in December 2010; the second was a transfer of muscles in his left arm (June 2011); the third, a de-rotation correction in his left femur bone (April 2013); and the fourth, a plate removal surgery (April 2015). Due to surgeries and treatment, his education fell behind, resulting in slower progress compared to his classmates.

In the mainstream school, my son experienced lack of participation and involvement. For surgery and follow-up, we had to take him to Kasturba Medical College, Manipal – an eleven hour journey by train. Moreover, the special orthotic devices he received from a child development centre in the UK – AFO (ankle–foot orthosis) from hip to toe to avoid scoliosis and internal rotation and a lycra suit to keep his body intact – are not available in India. The change in the circumstances had psychological effects in my son; he longed to study in a school in the UK (he cherished the memories of good support and education he received there). Based on our experience of facing challenges and difficulties, we've come to appreciate the importance of timely support, guidance, and encouragement for parents navigating the journey with a child who has special needs.

This made my husband and me think about starting a facility in our local area for children with special needs and their families. From those thoughts came the innovative work of Deepti Special School and Rehabilitation Centre – supporting, caring, educating, and addressing the specific needs of children with disabilities and their families, with a vision to equip, empower, and motivate them.

Feeling Different: Affirming Identity

When Jyothish was twelve years old he asked me the question, "Why was I born like this?" He was (and is) a very good, charming boy and was beginning to develop critical thoughts. From nine months of age, he had undergone many treatments and he found it very hard to cope with the pain and difficulties. He did not express his emotions until he was eight years old, but then he began to show discomfort with the surgeries and treatment system he was going through, which also reduced his learning pace. Those four surgeries in five years made him enquire why he was undergoing suffering in his body. He looked at his friends and his brothers and identified one significant matter that made him different – his disability. He commented, "I should not have been born." I asked him to look at the children at Deepti Centre and how they are affected with disability. He replied, "I pray that God would have made everyone normal, quite normal." I understood normalcy is what he sought. His problem was his limitations and restricted movement, and he wanted complete deliverance from it.

Disability and Families

Parents of children with disability also struggle to find answers to the question regarding why innocent children suffer in this world. We often see a similar question in Psalms, "Why do the righteous suffer?" I wonder if these parents can understand the language of the "thorn in the flesh." What about those who are of other faiths? How can they understand the Lord's answer to Paul? How can a person think that their suffering will bring good when they see no hope of good in their future? They begin in suffering and end in suffering. I know a family from the other faiths,[5] who had a child with severe disability who lived till ten years of age but was quite underdeveloped. He was their first born and passed away, due to pneumonia. The mother could not cope with the death of her child, and she could not have another child due to her health issues – she committed suicide after six months. Her health issues started with childbearing and this situation drove her into depression. I met another lady who had a child with a disability who said, "I do not believe in God because innocent children are suffering." In another family the husband left his wife because of the birth of a disabled child; later, he committed suicide. The mother was an active member of our Deepti family, and her child received treatment and care.

The all-sufficient grace and power in weakness is an essential matter when living in an ongoing crisis. It is always difficult to find an answer as Paul did, especially one that leads one to come to terms with whatever thorn buffets them. Has everyone reached the spiritual maturity of Paul? Can everyone have a vision of the crucified Christ and hear the voice of him who empowers and enables? At Deepti Special School, we have families of different faiths.

---

5. These are the common struggles people are undergoing irrespective of their faith in God. However the way each person respond to the struggles is different.

However, the way they share their stories of how Deepti Centre helps them to proceed in their journey with a child with disability is quite amazing. They used to cry and look down upon themselves for having a child with disability. But the fellowship of warmth, love and affection we have with each other helps them be strong.

As a mother of a child with disability, many times I have been very low. This may be the situation of parents who have differently abled children. But whenever I face such situations, I have visions and dreams that strengthen me in this journey of looking after my child responsibly by giving him the best care I can in this world. The power I receive from God is what I share with the community I work with so that they are strengthened. It is possible as we go through pain and suffering to see it as an opportunity to receive comfort from God. Those who undergo real pain often see that what they can offer to those who are in similar crises can make a positive change. The example of Deepti Centre is this. I experienced the pain and suffering of a mother who has a child with special needs, with the result that I could understand the problems faced by families having children with disabilities. The affliction and sufferings I passed through inspired me to start a service for the families having children with special needs. I saw a divine purpose behind the crises and approached these as an opportunity to receive comfort from God and pass on that comfort to others. Now Jyothish has finished his Bachelors of Design in Communication Design from Presidency University. Looking back through the years, I would say that, at every moment, I received Christ's power to go forward without giving up. The sufferings helped me empathize with those who are facing similar crises and give mutual support and mutual care and love to others.

From Sight to Insight

Deepti Special School and Rehabilitation Centre

The Deepti Centre for Children with Cerebral Palsy (renamed as Deepti Rehabilitation Centre) was established on 19 August 2009 and Deepti Special School was founded on 10 August 2010, in Manakala, Kerala, India.[6] Deepti is now an example of how an organisation can be like a family. My PhD thesis was

---

6. In 2009, I received a travel fund from Durham University to organise my trip to my hometown, Kerala. In 2010, I received funds from Durham Graduate School to do training at Villa Real School (in Consett, County Durham, UK) and for organizing a conference on special education in Kerala. The care and support that my child received at Durham and the training and experiences I gathered during my studies at Durham University made a significant contri-

about mutuality and women's ministry, based on exegetical work on Romans 16:1–16. This study helped me understand more of Paul's exhortations regarding love and support to one another and how to honour others. The story of a person overcoming crises is always an encouraging one and people like to hear such experiences of success. At Deepti, people undergoing similar crises come under one roof for fellowship, love, support, encouragement, and care. As they undergo suffering together, they may mutually benefit through growing in some good character qualities. Patience is one important quality that parents can develop by looking after a child with special needs. Hope is another quality people in suffering need to cherish on this journey, since a person without hope can give up at any time. I have heard from parents that some medical doctors openly tell them that there is no hope for their child affected with disability and, hence, they should prioritize looking after and educating those children in the family born without disability. This type of comment can be a significant blow to the parents and affect them psychologically, leading to depression, family problems, irresponsibility, lack of care giving, suicide, etc. In such scenarios, our efforts at Deepti in leading parents to a new vision of the world's reality are all the more important, whether those efforts involve giving advice to the parents of children with disability, showing how they can take care of the child, or demonstrating and supporting in the ways possible that will contribute to the child's survival.

Deepti aims at developing individual capacities by empowering children, integrating family values, and enlightening communities. The motto of the organisation is "Enabling the Present, Enlightening the Future" and its mission is "committed to be the most preferred special education centre through professional excellence, child centricity, and passionate service. The core values of Deepti are: care with love; support with acceptance; affirmation of dignity; education with understanding; maximization of every talent; holistic development; acknowledgement of every gift; and family focus. Initially set up to support children with CP, the Deepti Centre now provides services to more than 200 children with various physical and intellectual challenges. The staff now include special educators, support staff, therapists, and drivers.

Features of Deepti
Persons with disabilities comprise at least 4 to 8 percent of the Indian population. Children with disabilities in India are subject to multiple deprivations

---

bution to my ability to support the families who have children with special needs in my home country.

and limited opportunities in several dimensions of their lives. Their families and caregivers also go through a lot of stress and challenges in having a person with disability at home which ultimately leads to grave discriminatory practices towards these children.[7] Those living in rural villages, are often without education, medical care, proper food, and clothing. Under these circumstances, the education and support services at Deepti Special School and Rehabilitation Centre are unique in their quality.

Deepti follows an integrative model – a combination of services by medical experts, therapists, and special educators with the active involvement of family and community. Partnership and networking are also very important for Deepti to gain and exchange ideas, information, and knowledge for the improvement of the life condition of the families and children with special needs. The services rendered at the Deepti Centre and the Special School are early intervention; special education; speech therapy; physiotherapy; occupational therapy; creative play; vocational training; counselling; extracurricular activities such as instrumental music, sports, dance, music, art and band. Deepti has qualified, experienced, and committed staff; an innovative curriculum; open school examination; special toys; interactive electronic games; audio visual aids; a sensory room; a well-equipped physiotherapy gym; guidance and support for parents; workshops and seminars; etc.

Deepti continues to develop long-standing relationships with individuals and organizations in different countries and also contributes to the development of a team of international educational experts and medical specialists assisting children with special needs in Kerala. Deepti is committed to promoting dignity and quality of life in the experience of children with disability by developing individual capacity, family involvement, and community participation. Local community members are invited to join in during special programmes, exhibitions, awareness programmes, and celebrations at Deepti. Their participation provides them with glimpses of what is happening at Deepti and makes them aware of attitudinal changes the community needs to have towards children with special needs and their families for further positive steps to integrate their lives with the mainstream of the society.

The most rewarding thing of all is the improvement that we see in children after they join Deepti – along with the great sense of aspiration for a bright future for their children in the hearts of their parents. The Deepti family keeps growing, as do the dreams of children and parents who are very much part of

---

7. https://www.ncbi.nlm.nih.gov/pmc/articles/PMC4367071/ accessed on 29 September 2016.

it. Many parents have brought their children to the Deepti Special School and Rehabilitation Centre after hearing from other parents about the improvements of their children. Parents from distant places have rented houses near Deepti School to avail the excellent services and special education for their children.

Deepti is bringing a light of hope to families groping in the dark regarding their child's future possibilities as they wrestle with the realities of life; and it is impacting a wider community to love and serve others. Here I quote Jean Vanier,

> To love someone does not mean first of all to do things for that person; it means helping one to discover her own beauty, uniqueness, the light hidden in her heart and the meaning of her life. Through love a new hope is communicated to that person and thus desire to live and to grow. This communication of love requires words, but love is essentially communicated through non-verbal means: our attitudes, eyes, our gestures, and our smiles.[8]

---

8. Jean Vanier, *Tears of Silence* (London: Darton, Longman, and Todd, 1997), 5.

7

Enabling Grace: Towards a Holistic Vision

Perspectives in Question: Healing and Non-Healing

What is our response when our prayers are not answered? Does it affect our faith? Does it alter our perspective about God? What happens when we receive ill treatment from others? Does it affect our life-goals and mission? These are the issues I faced in my journey with a child with special needs. I came to the realization that every human being is unique, and God has a very special and unique purpose and plan regarding each and every one. It is our perspective that needs to be refined and reviewed on the basis of our life experiences. We live in a world of realities – one way or the other. Sickness, illness, and suffering may not be a punishment for sin. The ideas of normalcy or normative biases always push a few to the fringes of community.

Diversity enriches Christ's body, making it functional, and enhances the beauty and admiration of the world. When we embrace the beauty of diversity and recognize its benefits, we can appreciate the creative artistry of our Creator. Viewing individuals with disabilities as integral parts of the body opens our eyes, providing insight through understanding. Those whom society often labels as "less fortunate" can offer love and valuable gifts to those deemed "more fortunate," and vice versa. It's crucial to remember that people with disabilities are also created by God and therefore recipients of his gifts. This mutual sharing of love and gifts reflects God's design for the world, demonstrating the truth of his kingdom among us.

God's kingdom embodies love, peace, joy, fellowship, justice, and the integrity of all people. Embracing diversity and recognizing the inherent value in every individual allows us to witness and participate in the manifestation of God's kingdom here on earth.

Benefits of a "Thorn in the Flesh": Reimagining Theology and Ministry

Paul's perspective on suffering, as expressed in Corinthians, was profoundly shaped by his intimate fellowship with Jesus Christ and his experience of Christ's grace. These influences instilled in him a sense of humility and a keen awareness of his own vulnerability, dependence, and generosity.[1] He readily identified with Christ's suffering, treated others with mutual respect and support, and willingly accepted the humility of being regarded as the foremost of sinners. Instead of boasting about his own abilities or knowledge, Paul embraced his role as a servant and steward of the gospel.

Paul was acutely conscious of his susceptibility to sin and his inability to rely solely on his own strength. He understood that his perseverance in faith and hope for eschatological salvation depended entirely on the power of Christ's resurrection and his solidarity with Christ's sufferings. Paul's weaknesses and limitations served as a conduit for God's power to manifest itself in his ministry, highlighting his complete dependence on divine strength.

Moreover, Paul's experiences of suffering fostered in him a gracious attitude toward others, particularly those who stumbled or caused him grief. His encounters with adversity taught him empathy and compassion, enabling him to extend grace to those in need. In summary, Paul's understanding of suffering was not just theoretical but deeply personal and transformative. It shaped his identity as a follower of Christ, a steward of the gospel, and a compassionate advocate for those facing hardships. His humility, vulnerability, and reliance on God's strength exemplify his profound spiritual journey and commitment to spreading the message of grace and redemption.

Theology of the Cross

Paul's perspective in theology had a new phase ever since his conversion: the sovereign God became a servant God and co-sufferer in the incarnate Jesus Christ. This new understanding of God's power, manifested through the powerlessness of Christ on the cross, subverted all human understanding of power and weakness. Thus, the all-sufficiency of God's grace is acknowledged in suffering, which he experienced through his "thorn in the flesh." In other words, Paul also understood the divine agency that works through the experience of

---

1. See Don N. Howell, "Paul's Theology of Suffering," In *Paul's Missionary Methods: In His Time and Ours*, ed. by R. L. Plummer and J. M. Terry (England: IVP, 2012), 101–5.

human brokenness and suffering to bring about transformation and empowerment for the one who trusts in Christ.

Cruciform Ministry

Paul's experience of suffering enabled him in many ways. It enriched his perspectives and ideals, brought him closer to Christ, deepened his understanding of the cross of Christ, and increased his reliance on Christ's power. The cross of Christ left a permanent mark in his life and ministry. It enabled him to strengthen others with the same enabling he received from God. Because that enabling did not end in Paul himself, but flowed from him to others, it brought glory to the name of God. Paul found a divine goal in his suffering – to be a vessel for transferring God's consolation and compassion. One who has experienced hardships can more easily identify with the problems of others. Moreover, those who are suffering may also identify with those who have experienced similar crisis, and hence they may open up more freely to those people.

Renewed "Self-Understanding"

Paul understood the dividing line between boasting in one's personal achievements and boasting in one's weaknesses. His personhood was completely changed; he was refined and renewed to reach out to yet another group of people with similar experiences to his. An illness may have been an obstacle to missionary work; instead, for Paul, yet another huge door was opened up for mission. Those who look through this lens will see the dual images of Paul and of Christ: Paul being weakened and, at the same time, Christ uniquely pouring out his grace and power, enabling and empowering others. Everyone has their own experience of knowing Christ and experiencing his power; their experiences are not always the same. Although the same God and same Spirit is working in everyone, there is a diversity of encounters with God. This is an important matter to understand in one's spiritual journey and mission. We all possess one vision, one motif, one mission in God, one Lord, and the one Spirit who acknowledges unity, however, when it comes to our roles in the world, these are fulfilled through differences in people, visions, motives, and mission though all pertain to the One God who is the Maker and the Creator. This perspective changed Paul from self-reliant to God-reliant.

Paul's vision of enabling grace and power is unique. What he had experienced is little known to us, but it is clear that he prayed and moved closer to God and even received grace to withstand God's answer – non-removal of suffering. This is often the point where a believer finds it hard to cope and begins questioning: "Why do bad things happen to good people? Why do innocent children suffer?"

I consider here adults and children with intellectual disabilities who have limited understanding and little power to be self-motivated. By giving early training, carers or mothers can change the life-situation of people with severe life conditions. Although it is tiring and disappointing sometimes, the slogan "try, try, always try" can change life situations from a negative to a positive one, from rejection to acceptance, and from dying to living.

The Power of the Enabling Grace

The word "grace' is frequently used in the Pauline literature. He uses this significant term in different contexts such as salvation, gifts, in contrast to the law, in greetings and benedictions, etc. Two important interrelated questions arise from these contexts. First, what are the different notions of grace in the Pauline epistles? Second, what is the meaning of grace in relation to disability?

In 1 Corinthians 15:10, grace was what transformed Paul from a persecutor of Christ to his messenger and sustained all that he undertook as Christ's servant: "By the grace of God, I am what I am." Furthermore, grace is a gift from God and its effect in daily living is important. In 2 Corinthians 12:7–10, grace was the aid that enabled Paul to suffer the thorn in his personal life and which benefited him with the power that is made perfect in weakness. Paul spoke about grace in his ministry, grace in proclamation, grace in daily living with Christ; he related all activities of a Christian to God's grace. More significant for those who are disabled is that the grace and power of God were sufficient in Paul's life of weakness. "My grace is sufficient for you and my power is made perfect in weakness" means that there is an infilling of God's enabling and strength when one is weak and powerless.

Family, Church, and Society Perspectives on Disability: Response and Responsibility

Family, church and society each have great influence in the lives of persons with disability. Disability varies in degrees and types; equally, the environment in which disability arises can make impactful differences in the everyday lives of people living with it. Families, society, and the church can build barriers shutting people with disability out or find ways to build bridges towards those with disability and make their lives easier. Societies based on competition for power, money, and status may blind our eyes towards the people who are in need and who are on the fringes of society. People may not think about others unless or until they suffer or undergo similar disability and difficulty. Selfishness and egocentrism have negative effects on others, especially those who are suffering and in need. Furthermore, the notions of people regarding disability vary hugely: the persons with disability can be seen either as angels or devils; as a blessing or a curse; as the will of God or a punishment for sin; as a test of faith or an opportunity for character development; as a manifestation of the power of God or redemptive suffering. Others prefer to regard disability within God's mysterious omnipotence.[2]

Another issue that affects the lives of people with disabilities is the willingness of families, society and churches to recognize and respect others who are different from us. The mode of acceptance and welcome in Christian communities should be more significant than in communities of other faiths, especially when people with disability are struggling to find their identity in the society and parents are struggling to discover even minimal care for their disabled children. A theology of mutuality gives significance to all as the persons with disability and those without disability seek to benefit each other, support each other, and learn from each other.

Family and Disability

The family of a child with disability includes not only the parents and the siblings but the extended family. The family environment in which a disabled child grows up makes rather a big difference to the growth of that child. Where there are not enough facilities and awareness within society, the needs of adults and children with disabilities may be met within supportive and caring families. Wider family members can support the parents and siblings of a disabled child or adult in dealing with the issues: they can spend time with the family, look after the disabled member, and provide the parents and/or siblings with time to relax or time out; they can also accompany them to the hospital and support them financially when needed.

---

2. Kathy Black, *A Healing Homiletic: Preaching and Disability* (Nashville: Abingdon, 1996), 19–33.

The Church

The church should be accessible, inclusive, welcoming, and hospitable communities of faith to the persons with disability. In the church, love is what we should receive from one another; as we receive it, we feel the warmth of it, and see what love is and looks like, embodied in our relationships. On a personal level, I remember when Jyothish had undergone his first surgery – tendon release on his legs – and had been in a cast for six weeks. During their visit to India in January 2011, Prof. John M. G. Barclay, my PhD supervisor, and his wife, Diana, spent time with us and read out stories to Jyothish. We often remember this time with joy and gratitude to God and to them. Being with others who are weak, vulnerable, and suffering is a way to show the love of Christ. It reminded me of the good Samaritan who loved by helping and serving the wounded.

"When people with disabilities are invited to join as full members, not just attend, they are being 're-membered' as part of the body of the people of faith."[3] The invitation to join is more than just relational; physical contexts also matter. Buildings should be physically accessible to people with disabilities. The church should build ramps and avoid barriers so that a person with movement-related disability can participate in the worship, however welcome and inclusion involve much more than physical access.

> Being accessible makes it possible for people to gain entry and join in. Being inclusive goes way beyond that, describing how we are as people – our attitude and approach to others, warmth of welcome of new arrivals, the encouragement and support given so that people can get most out of what church has to offer and can feel at home there.[4]

The Ecumenical Disability Advocates Network is a network and initiative of people with disabilities and is a WCC programme created to work with people with disabilities. WCC recognizes disability as a justice issue and the new

---

3. Bill Gaventa, "Signs of the Times: Theological Themes in the Changing Forms of Ministries and Spiritual Supports with People with Disabilities," *Disability Studies Quarterly* 26, no. 4 (2006): 5. I agree with Bill as he says, "If congregations truly are becoming communities of faith and worship where everyone's presence is welcomed and wanted, where pain is received and relieved, strengths sustained, gifts called forth and used, and vulnerabilities are seen not as a sign of sin, but as a reminder of the gift of grace that can work through all of God's people, then there really is a new era to celebrate . . . for all of us" (p. 10). See also William C. Gaventa, "Preaching disability: The whole of Christ's body in word and practice," *Review and Expositor* 113, no. 2 (2016): 225–42.

4. Tony Phelps-Jones, et.al., *Making Church Accessible to All: Including Disabled People in Church Life* (Croydon: CPI, 2013), 9.

interim statement, *A Church of All and for All*, stresses the role of churches in welcoming all for all are welcomed at God's banquet table.[5] It contains many prompts helping us consider how we can use each of the five human senses in gatherings and services to help people with disabilities to participate more fully.

Inclusive language and inclusive materials can be used in worship: different methods can be used in preaching to facilitate the understanding of biblical concepts to people with disabilities. Inclusive (and loving) churches consider questions about their methods that are often difficult to answer such as: how can we involve people with autism, sight loss, hearing loss, mobility difficulty, learning difficulty, mental issues, and those with additional needs? In our local church, a mother of an autistic and visually-impaired child shared the difficulty of attending the worship service with her son since he had the tendency to run towards the pulpit to reach towards the sound. After discussions with specialists in autism, we read out social stories that help her son understand the situation around him and respond accordingly.

Despite the practical difficulties, each church has to acknowledge people with disabilities are part of the body of Christ, part of that local church, and willingly accept their gifts and that they are also part of the church. The local church should be a place of acceptance and comfort for people with disabilities and a place where isolation, shunning, stereotyping, discrimination, and exclusion do not exist.[6] The attitude of people in the local church should resemble that of Jesus, who recognised and accepted others. If we disregard those with disabilities, we disregard those for whom Christ has died. As Paul says, "Yes everything is for your sake, so that grace, as it extends to more and more people, may increase thanksgiving, to the glory of God" (2 Cor 4:15).

Society

For wider society to become more inclusive and supportive of people with disabilities, it needs to follow the participatory model. The education and training of children with disabilities are important factors that can change their lives. Society can assist families supporting members with disabilities by: opening up rehabilitation centres or day care centres; providing the family and the

---

5. World Council of Churches (Geneva, Switzerland), 26 August – 2 September 2003. See also, Anne Fritzon and Samuel Kabue, *Interpreting Disability: A Church of All and for All* (Geneva: WCC, 2004), 59, 60.

6. For a discussion on Ecclesiology in a disability perspective, see Mathew C. Vargheese, "Re-visioning Ecclesia from a Disability Perspective," in *Faith and Vision: A Festschrift in Honour of Rev. Dr. T. G. Koshy*, edited by T. M. Jose (Manakala: FTS, 2022), 165–92.

child with regular counselling; being aware of the need for timely care; and assisting with transportation of a disabled child to school or to the hospital in case of treatment. However, in developing countries, especially in rural areas and slums, there are a few or no facilities for the education of children with disabilities. Thus, society members can make a significant contribution by bringing awareness of these areas of need to the government. Governments can make funds available for starting such services in order to provide the persons with disabilities with access to education and services.

Another way by which society can support those with disabilities is to give them employment in public sectors. Finding their hidden talents and enabling them to use their skills for the benefit of the whole society contributes to their well-being and society's. Finally, society also should work against the social evils (abuse, discrimination, de-motivation, mockery) that hinder the development of people with disability and the inequality between their rights and the rights of those without disabilities. The enactment of laws in favour of those with disabilities can also be supported by society.

The Story of Arthur and Frances

I came across a book authored by Frances Young when writing my current book. *Arthur's Call*[7] is Frances's autobiography. It tells her journey of faith with her son, Arthur: from grief to gratitude, from anxiety to hope, from trauma to trust, and from anguish to joy. It resonated to a great extent with my own experience of being a minister and a mother of a child with special needs. Arthur was born in 1967, severely brain damaged, unable to learn to do anything for himself, and consequently dependent on other people for his every need. His mother, Frances, is a Methodist minister and former Edward Cadbury Professor of Theology in the University of Birmingham. Arthur lived at home for forty-five years, cared by his own parents, and then moved into full-time professional care.

Frances's words as she faced the reality of life as a mother of a child with profound disability are meaningful for people who are also undergoing similar crises.

---

7. Frances Young, *Arthur's Call: A Journey of Faith in the Face of Severe Learning Disability* (London: SPCK, 2014), ix. See also Frances Young, ed. *Encounter with Mystery: Reflections on L'Arche and Living with Disability* (London: Darton, Longmann and Todd, 1997), 108; Frances Young, *Face to Face: A Narrative Essay in the Theology of Suffering* (Edinburgh: T&T Clark, 1990); Frances Young, *Brokenness and Blessing: Towards a Biblical Spirituality* (London: Darton, Longman and Todd, 2007).

> For years I'd struggled with questions in utter loneliness. It made me confess things I'd never shared with others before. The tragedy was not so much Arthur as my sense of abandonment, my inability to accept the existence and love of God at those deeper levels where it makes a real difference to one's life. I could still make a Christian confession; I still preached from time to time and often found that Wesley's advice, "Preach faith till you've got it," came true – that it was when I was giving to others, and only then, that I had any real grasp on what faith I had . . . But my experience was of an internal blank where God should've been. I had no hope for the future. Despair was lodged deep down inside even if, for the most part, I got on with life, and joked and played with the kids, and lectured in theology, and researched and wrote, passed for a Christian and went to church. Occasionally I'd wrestle with meaningless prayer to a blank wall. It did feel like a tragedy. Yet my friend's comment on the richness of my life came across as a healthy rebuke. It was after that evening that I began to climb out of my black hole and find release from the doubts and guilt, fears and self-concern that had imprisoned me.[8]

Her comment on the issue of healing as something miraculous happening to these children with disability is also significant.

> Suppose some faith healer laid hands on Arthur tomorrow and all his damaged brain cells were miraculously healed, what then? Brains gradually develop through learning. There are years of learning processes which Arthur missed out on . . . Arthur has personality at his own limited level. He has a mind of his own which can make his carers' lives a bit difficult. But I always found it impossible to envisage what it would mean for him to be healed . . . with all his limitations. Healed, he would be a different person.[9]

Here is the point where we have to redefine normalcy. "Normalcy" is the standard everyone looks to but accommodating "the other" is more important in a society of plurality and diversity. Acceptance and accommodation of differences and adaptation for the different circumstances of others helps society enjoy peace and justice.

---

8. Young, *Arthur's Call*, 28, 29.
9. Young, *Arthur's Call*, 34.

> By the broken body of Christ the body of humanity, are made whole.
> Our brokenness is the wound through which the power of God can penetrate our being and transfigure us in him.[10]

Love Crossing Cultural and Religious Barriers: Towards a Holistic Vision

God showed his unconditional love towards humankind through Jesus Christ, through brokenness, pain, and suffering. The suffering of Jesus Christ on the cross is significant for persons with disability in withstanding their suffering in this world. This is part of the ultimate will of God in sending his Son to the world: to bestow this gift of unconditional love to those who are unworthy and those who cannot even claim or speak out that they are worthy (namely, those who are intellectually disabled). "But God chose the foolish things of the world to shame the wise; God chose the weak things of the world to shame the strong. God chose the lowly things of this world and the despised things – and the things that are not – to nullify the things that are, so that no one may boast before him" (1 Cor 1:26–29). The good news of Jesus Christ, in other words, disregards all forms of human worth, it subverts every standard definition of symbolic value, because worth is not attributed according to human qualities or capacities, but according to one criterion only: it is bestowed by the love of God in Christ.[11]

It is good to think at this point about people of other faiths. The love of God is for all and not for a few who claim to be believers. The power and the grace of the cross is not limited to a specific group of people (those labelled as "Christians"). It is available to those who seek him irrespective of a particular religion, culture, race, caste, creed, gender, (dis)ability, power, or socio-economic status: "Christ died for all." Everyone is precious to God and thus we, as human beings, consider the worth of one another and love one another. This love starts from God through his Son, Jesus Christ; his love is given to all people, that they also may love one other. Loving is carrying burdens, giving time to others, suffering with others, sharing joy, and contributing to the needs

---

10. Young, *Arthur's Call*, 77. Frances quotes Jean Vanier who relates the fragility and brokenness of people with severe learning disabilities with the vulnerability and brokenness of Jesus Christ. See Jean Vanier, *The Broken Body: Journey to Wholeness* (London: Darton, Longman and Todd, 1988), 72.

11. J. M. G. Barclay, "Paul, Grace and Liberation from Human Judgments of Worth," *Mockingbird* 15 (2020): 57, 58.

of others. The price Jesus paid on the cross was his precious life; thus, the nature of the love shown in the cross is self-sacrificial.

> In Christ, our physical abilities or disabilities, weaknesses or strengths, size or shape, conformity or non-conformity to the standards of worth regnant in our culture do not matter: they do not matter to the God of grace, and they do not measure our worth . . . The only worth that counts is what we are given by the grace of God.[12]

God has created all for his purpose – no matter what kind of weakness or disability one has or not, the grace of Jesus Christ is sufficient in one's ongoing personal life. As the body of Christ, the community has the responsibility to love, support, care and encourage those who are weak, fragile and vulnerable, thus creating bonds of solidarity with those who are in need of mutual support.

Conclusion

This book stemmed from my own experience of having a child with disability and running a special school for children with various challenges. Pain and suffering in a person's life can lead to questioning the existence of God and his love and justice. The pain and suffering in my life led me to read Paul's perspective regarding suffering. The terms "weakness" and "thorn in the flesh" point to some kind of debilitating disease or condition, about which Paul asked God for healing. Rather than healing Paul from his unspecified condition, God filled Paul with his grace and power which enabled Paul to move on despite his weakness.

The way disability was viewed in antiquity was rather grim. Generally speaking, the experience of disability was viewed negatively. Many faced mockery and derision due to their physical deformity and disability. They were often abandoned or even killed. (The economic and career prospects of people with disability in antiquity varied, however, as a few had an independent status.) There was a popular view of disability as punishment from the gods. Judaism's calls for the priest's perfection in the Temple – priests needing to be without blemish, of pure lineage, and ritually pure – have a similar tendency to devalue people with disabilities.

Much of this book considers key sections of Paul's letter to the Corinthians. I have discussed the reversal of status in the kingdom of God, diversity in the

---

12. Barclay, "Paul, Grace and Liberation," 59.

members of the body of Christ, spiritual gifts and talents of people with disability, love encompassing weakness, and the place of people with disability in the resurrection and the nature of the resurrected body. I then discussed the components and highlights of Paul's view on suffering. Paul seems to have suffered with sickness, possibly something similar to a kind of disability since it was a continuing weakness. The grace that enabled him to cope with weakness is the most significant part of his life since, the more grace he needed, the weaker he was. How a person can, at the same time, be weak and strong is revealed in his catchphrase, "when I am weak, then I am strong." Having considered Paul's suffering, I then explained my personal journey of having a child with special needs: the ups and downs, the valleys and the mountains, the joys and the sorrows, the meaning and the meaninglessness, and the emptiness and the filling. I concluded this book by considering the implication and relevance of this study for the community of the disabled today.

Family, church, and society profoundly impact the lives of persons with disabilities. Each local church, representing God in its community, must strive to become accessible, inclusive, welcoming, and hospitable to people with disabilities. As part of the body of Christ, the church collectively bears the responsibility to love, support, care for, encourage, and embrace those who are frail, fragile and vulnerable. By fulfilling this role, we strengthen sacred bonds of solidarity through mutual support.

Bibliography

Abrams, Judith Z. *Judaism and Disability: Portrayals in Ancient Texts from the Tanach through the Balvi*. Washington, DC: Gallaudet University, 1998.

Albl, Martin. "For Whenever I am Weak, Then I am Strong: Disability in Paul's Epistles." In *This Abled Body: Rethinking Disabilities in Biblical Studies*. Eds. H. Avalos, S. J. Melcher and J. Schipper. Atlanta: SBL, 2007.

Anglican Church Great Britain, "Gospel and Spirit: A Joint Statement." In McDonnell (ed.), *Presence, Power and Praise: Documents on the Charismatic Renewal* 2 (Collegeville: Liturgical Press, 1980): 291–306.

Aristotle. *The Politics*. Translated by H. Rackham. LCL. Cambridge: Harvard University Press, 1944.

Arndt, W. F. and F. Wilbur Gingrich. *Greek–English Lexicon of the New Testament and Other Early Christian Literature*. London: University of Chicago, 1979.

Barclay, J. M. G. "Paul, Grace and Liberation from Human Judgments of Worth," *Mockingbird* 15 (2020): 50–61.

———. "Neither Jew Nor Greek: Multiculturalism and The New Perspective on Paul." In *Ethnicity and the Bible*. Ed. M. G. Brett. Leiden: Brill, 1996, 197–214.

Barnett, Paul. *The Second Epistle to the Corinthians*. NICNT. Grand Rapids: Eerdmans, 1997.

Barrett, C. K. *The First Epistle to the Corinthians*. London: A. & C. Black, 1968.

———. *A Commentary on the Second Epistle to the Corinthians*. London: A. & C. Black, 1973.

Barton, Carlin A. *The Sorrows of the Ancient Romans: The Gladiator and the Monster*. Princeton: Princeton University, 1993.

Bauer, W., W. F. Arndt, F. W. Gingrich and F. W. Danker. *Greek–English Lexicon of the New Testament and Other Early Christian Literature*, 3rd ed. London: University of Chicago, 2000.

Beyer. ἐπισκηνόω, TDNT 2nd ed. Gerhard Friedrich. Trans. & ed. Geoffrey W. Bromiley. Grand Rapids: Eerdmans, 1971, 599–622.

Black, D. A. "Weakness Language in Galatians."*Grace Theological Journal* no. 4 (1983): 15–36.

———. *Paul, Apostle of Weakness: Astheneia and its Cognates in the Pauline Literature*, rev. ed. Eugene: Pickwick Publications, 2012.

Black, Kathy. *A Healing Homiletic: Preaching and Disability*. Nashville: Abingdon, 1996.

Bohatec, J. "Inhalt und Reihenfolge der 'Schlagworte der Erlösungsreligion' in 1 Kor 1:26–31," 252–71.

Bonhoeffer, D. *Meditating on the Word*. Eng. trans. Cambridge: Cowley Publication, 1986.

———. *Christology*. Eng. trans. London: SCM, 1978.

———. *The Communion of the Saints: A Dogmatic Inquiry into the Sociology of the Church*. Eng. trans. New York: Harper & Row, 1963.

———. *Ethics*. New York: Macmillan, 1965.

———. *The Cost of Discipleship*. London: SCM, 2001.

Bowie, E. L. "The Importance of the Sophists." *Yale Classical Studies* 27 (1982): 28–59.

Bruce, F. F. *1 and 2 Corinthians*. NCBC. London: Oliphants, 1971.

Bultmann, R. *Theology of the New Testament*. Waco: Baylor, 2007.

Buxton, R. G. A. "Blindness and Limits: Sophocles and the Logic of Myth." *The Journal of Hellenic Studies* 100 (1980): 22–37.

Calvin, J. *The First Epistle of Paul the Apostle to the Corinthians*. Edinburgh: Oliver & Boyd, 1960.

Charles, R. H. *Apocrypha and Pseudepigrapha of the OT, II*. 2 vols., Oxford: Clarendon, 1913, 2:508.

Chrysostom, J. *Homilies on the Epistle of Paul to the Corinthians*. English NPNF. Ed. P. Schaff. Edinburgh: T&T Clark, 1887–94; Grand Rapids: Eerdmans, 1989, 1–269.

Cicero, M. Tullius. *De Officiis*. Translated by Walter Miller. Cambridge: Harvard University, 1913.

Collins, R. F. *1 Corinthians*. Sacra Pagina 7. Collegeville: Liturgical, 1999.

Conzelmann, H. *1 Corinthians: A Commentary*. Hermeneia. Eng. trans. Philadelphia: Fortress, 1975.

Craig, C. T. *The First Epistle to the Corinthians*. IB, 10. New York: Nashville: Abingdon, 1953.

Davies, W. D. *Paul and Rabbinic Judaism: Some Rabbinic Elements in Pauline Theology*. 2nd ed. London: SPCK, 1958.

Davis, J. A. *Wisdom and Spirit*. New York: University Press of America, 1984.

Deissmann, G. A. *Light from the Ancient Near East*. London: Hodder & Stoughton, 2nd ed. 1927.

———. *Paul: A Study in Social and Religious History*. Eng. trans. 2nded. London: Hodder & Stoughton, 1926.

Delling, G. σκόλοψ. TDNT 7. Ed. Gerhard Friedrich; trans. and ed. Geoffrey W. Bromiley. Grand Rapids: Eerdmans, 1971, 409–424.

Deluz, V. G. A. *Companion to 1 Corinthians*. London: DLT, 1963.

den Boer, W. *Private Morality in Greece and Rome: Some Historical Aspects*. Leiden: Brill, 1979.

DeSilva, D. A. "Let the One who Claims Honor Establish that Claim in the Lord: Honor Discourse in the Corinthian Correspondence." *BTB* 28 (1998): 61–74.

Dill, Samuel. *Roman Society in the Last Century of the Western Empire*. London: Macmillan, 1900.

Dio Chrysostom. *Orations*. Translated by J. W. Cohoon. London: Heinemann, 1932.

Dionysius of Halicarnassus. *Roman Antiquities, Volume II: Books 3–4*. Translated by Earnest Cary. LCL 347. Cambridge: Harvard University, 1939.

Douglas, Mary. *Purity and Danger: An Analysis of Concepts of Pollution and Taboo.* New York: Praeger, 1966.

Dunn, J. D. G. *The Theology of the Apostle Paul.* Grand Rapids: Eerdmans, 1998.

———. *Jesus and the Spirit: A Study of the Religious and Charismatic Experience of Jesus and the First Christians as Reflected in the New Testament.* London: SCM, 1965.

Epictetus. *His Discourses. In Four Books.* Translated by Thomas Wentworth Higginson. New York: Thomas Nelson and Sons, 1890.

Fee, Gordon, *God's Empowering Presence: the Holy Spirit in the Letters of Paul.* Grand Rapids: Baker Books, 2009.

———. *The First Epistle to the Corinthians.* Grand Rapids: Eerdmans, 1987.

Ferguson, J. *The Religions of the Roman Empire.* New York: Cornell University, 1970.

Finley, M. I. *The Ancient Economy.* Berkeley: University of California, 1973.

Fitzgerald, John T. *Cracks in an Earthen Vessel An Examination of the Catalogues of Hardships in the Corinthian Correspondence.* SBLDS 99. Atlanta: Scholars, 1988.

Fritzon, Anne, and Samuel Kabue. *Interpreting Disability: A Church of All and for All.* Geneva: WCC, 2004.

Fuchs, E. "La faiblesse, gloire de l'apostolat selon Paul. Étudesur 2 Corinthiens 10–13." *ETR* 5 (1980): 231–53.

Garland, D. E. *1 Corinthians.* BECNT. Grand Rapids: Baker Academic, 2003.

Garland, Robert. "The Mockery of the Deformed and Disabled in Graeco–Roman Culture." In *Laughter Down the Centuries*, Vol 1. Edited by Siegfried Jakel and Asko Timonen. Turku: TurunYliopsto, 1994.

———. *Eye of the Beholder: Deformity and Disability in the Greco-Roman World.* London: Duckworth, 1995.

Garnsey, P. *Social Status and Legal Privilege in the Roman Empire.* Oxford: The Clarendon, 1970.

Gaventa, Bill. "Signs of the Times: Theological Themes in the Changing Forms of Ministries and Spiritual Supports with People with Disabilities. On-line journal, *Disability Studies Quarterly* 26, no. 4 (2006): 1–10.

Gaventa, William C. "Preaching Disability: The Whole of Christ's Body in Word and Practice." *Review and Expositor* 113, no. 2 (2016): 225–42.

Glad, C. E. *Paul and Philodemus: Adaptability in Epicurean and Early Christian Psychology.* NovTSup, 81; Leiden: Brill, 1995.

Godet, F. L. *Commentary on the First Epistle of St. Paul to the Corinthians.* Vol. 2, chs. 9–16. Translated by A. Cusin. Edinburgh: T&T Clark, 1887.

Goudge, H. L. *The First Epistle to the Corinthians.* 3rd ed. Westminster Commentaries. London: Methuen, 1911.

Grant, Frederick C. *Roman Hellenism and the New Testament.* New York: Charles Scribner's Sons, 1962.

Grmek, Mirko D. *Diseases in the Ancient Greek World.* Translated by Mireille Muellner and Leonard Muellner. Baltimore: Johns Hopkins University, 1989.

Grudem, Wayne. *Systematic Theology: An Introduction to Biblical Doctrine.* Secunderabad: OM Books, 2003.
Grundmann. "δύναμαι." TDNT 2nd ed. Edited by Gerhard Kittel. Translated and edited Geoffrey W. Bromiley. Grand Rapids: Eerdmans, 1964, 284–317.
Harris, Murray J. *The Second Epistle to the Corinthians.* NIGTC. Grand Rapids: Eerdmans, 2013.
Herodotus, *Histories.* Translated LCL by A. D. Godley. London: Heinnemann, 1920.
Homer. *The Illiad.* Translated by R. Lattimore. Chicago: University of Chicago, 1951.
———. *The Odyssey.* 2 vols. LCL. Translated by A. T. Murray. Cambridge: Harvard University, 1919.
Hornblower, Simon, and Anthony Spawforth, (eds.). *The Oxford Classical Dictionary.* 3rd Ed. Oxford and New York: Oxford University, 1996.
Horrell, D. G. *The Social Ethos of the Corinthian Correspondence: Interest and Ideology from 1 Corinthians to 1 Clement.* Edinburgh: T&T Clark, 1996.
Horsley, R. A. *1 Corinthians.* Nashville: Abingdon, 1998.
Howell, Don N, Jr. "Paul's Theology of Suffering." In *Paul's Missionary Methods: In His Time or Ours.* Edited by John Robert, L. Plummer and John Mark Terry. Leicester: Inter-Varsity Press, 2012.
Hughes, P. E. *Paul's Epistle to the Corinthians.* NICNT. Grand Rapids: Eerdmans, 1961.
Jeremias, J. "Flesh and Blood Cannot Inherit the Kingdom of God." *NTS* 2 (1995–56): 151–59.
Jewett, R. *Paul's Anthropological Terms.* Leiden: Brill, 1971.
Judge, E. A. *The Social Pattern of the Christian Groups in the First Century.* London: Tyndale, 1960.
Jungel, E. *God as the Mystery of the World: On the Foundation of the Theology of the Crucified One in the Dispute between Theism and Atheism.* London: Bloomsbury, 2014.
———. *Theological Essays.* Eng. trans. Edinburgh: T&T Clark, 1989.
Käsemann, E. "The Theological Problem Presented by the Motif of the Body of Christ." In *Perspectives on Paul.* London: SCM, 1971, 102–21.
Kelley, N. "Deformity and Disability in Greece and Rome." In *This Abled Body: Rethinking Disabilities in Biblical Studies.* Edited by H. Avalos, S. J. Melcher and J. Schipper. Atlanta: SBL, 2007, 31–46.
Kennedy, H. A. A. *St. Paul's Conceptions of the Last Things.* London: Paternoster, 1904.
Kistemaker, S. J. *1 Corinthians.* NTC. Grand Rapids: Baker Books, 1993.
Lakoff, George. *Women, Fire and Dangerous Things: What Categories Reveal about Mind.* Chicago: University of Chicago, 1987.
Liddell, H. G., R. Scott and H. S. Jones. *A Greek–English Lexicon.* 9th ed. with revised supplement. Oxford: Oxford University, 1996.
Link, H. G. "Weakness" (ἀσθένεια) in Colin Brown (ed.), *New Testament Theology Vol. 3: Pri–Z.* Exeter: Paternoster, 1978, 993–96.

Luther, Martin. *Luther's Works. Commentaries on 1 Corinthians 7 and 1 Corinthians 15*, vol. 28. St. Louis: Concordia, 1973, 9–214 (WA, 12:97–142 and 36:482–696).
———. *Early Theological Works*. Translated and edited by J. Atkinson. London: SCM, 1962.
MacMullen, R. *Roman Social Relations*. London: Yale University, 1974.
———. *Enemies of the Roman Order: Treason, Unrest, and Alienation in the Empire*. Cambridge: Harvard University, 1967.
Martin, D. "Tongues of Angels and Other Status Indicators." *JAAR* 59 (1991): 547–89.
———. *The Corinthian Body*. New Haven: Yale University, 1995.
Martin, R. P. *2 Corinthians*. WBC 40. Waco: Word Books, 1986.
McCloughry, Roy, and Wayne Morris. *Making a World of Difference: Christian Reflections on Disability*. London: SPCK, 2002.
Meeks, W. A. *The Moral World of the First Christians*. Louisville: Westminster John Knox, 1986.
———. *The First Urban Christians: The Social World of the Apostle Paul*. New Haven and London: Yale University, 1983.
Meyer, H. A. W. *Critical and Exegetical Handbook to the Epistle to the Corinthians*. Eng. trans., 2 vols. Edinburgh: T&T Clark, 1892, 1:37.
Mitchell, M. M. "Rhetorical Shorthand in Pauline Argumentation: The Function of "the Gospel' in the Corinthian Correspondence." In *Gospel in Paul: Studies on Corinthians, Galatians and Romans for R. N. Longenecker*. Edited by L. A. Jervis and P. Richardson, JSNT Supplement Series 108. Sheffield: Sheffield Academic, 1994, 65.
Moffatt, J. *The First Epistle of Paul to the Corinthians*. Moffatt New Testament Commentary 7. London: Hodder & Stoughton, 1938.
Moltmann, J. *The Crucified God*. Trans. R. A. Wilson and John Bowden. London: SCM, 1975.
———. *The Way of Jesus Christ*. Minneapolis: Fortress, 1995.
———. *Theology of Hope*. Eng. trans. London: SCM, 1967.
———. "The Knowing of the Other and the Community of the Different." In *God for a Secular Society*. Eng. trans. London: SCM, 1999.
O'Connor, J. Murphy. *The Theology of the Second Letter to the Corinthians*. Cambridge: Cambridge University, 1991.
Petronius. *Satyricon*. Translated by Sarah Ruden. Indianapolis: Hackett, 2000.
Phelps-Jones, Tony. *Making Church Accessible to All: Including Disabled People in Church Life*. Croydon: CPI, 2013.
Plato. *The Republic*. 2 vols. Translated by P. Shorey. LCL. Cambridge: Harvard University, 1953.
Pliny. *Natural History*. Translated by John Bostock and H. T. Riley. London: York, 1855.
Plutarch. *Moralia*. Harold North Fowler, trans. 14 vols. LCL. Cambridge: Harvard University, 1927.
Pogoloff, S. M. *Logos and Sophia: The Rhetorical Structure of 1 Corinthians*. Society of Biblical Literature Dissertation Series 134. Atlanta: Scholars, 1992.

Robertson, A., and A. Plummer. *A Critical and Exegetical Commentary on the First Epistle of Paul to the Corinthians*. ICC. Edinburgh: T&T Clark, 1914.

Robinson, A. T. *The Body: A Study in the Pauline Theology*. London: SCM, 1957.

Rose, Martha L. *The Staff of Oedipus: Transforming Disability in Ancient Greece*. Ann Arbor: University of Michigan, 2003.

Sand, A. σάρξ. *EDNT*. Edited by H. Balz and G. Schneider. 3 vols. Grand Rapids: Eerdmans, 1990–93.

Savage, Timothy B. *Power through Weakness: Paul's Understanding of the Christian Ministry in 2 Corinthians*. SNTS Monograph Series. Cambridge: Cambridge University, 1996.

Schlier, Heinrich. θλῖψις. *TDNT* 3. Edited by Gerhard Kittel, translated and edited Geoffrey W. Bromiley. Grand Rapids: Eerdmans, 1965, 143–48.

Schmidt, K. L. κολαφίζω. *TDNT* 3. Edited by Gerhard Kittel, translated and edited Geoffrey W. Bromiley. Grand Rapids: Eerdmans, 1965, 818–21.

Schmitz, O., and G. Stahlin. παράκλησις. *TDNT* 5. Edited by Gerhard Friedrich. Translated and edited by Geoffrey W. Bromiley. Grand Rapids: Eerdmans, 1967, 773–93.

Schmitz, O. παρακαλέω, *TDNT* 5. Edited by Gerhard Friedrich. Translated and edited by Geoffrey W. Bromiley. Grand Rapids: Eerdmans, 1967, 793–799.

Schweitzer, A. *The Mysticism of Paul the Apostle*. Translated by W. Montgomery. London: Black, 1931.

Schweitzer, E. σάρξ. *TDNT* 7. Edited by Gerhard Friedrich. Translated and edited by Geoffrey W. Bromiley. Grand Rapids: Eerdmans, 125–36.

Seneca. *Epistles, Volume I: Epistles 1–65*. Translated by Richard Gummere. LCL 75. Cambridge: Harvard University, 1917.

Seneca the Elder. *Declamations, Volume II: Controversiae, Books 7–10. Suasoriae. Fragments*. Translated by Michael Winterbottom. LCL 464. Cambridge: Harvard University, 1974.

Soards, M. L. *1 Corinthians*. NIBC. Peabody: Hendrickson, 1999.

Soranus. *Gynaecology*. Translated by Owsei Temkin. Baltimore: John Hopkins, 1956.

Stowers, S. K. "Paul on the Use and Abuse of Reason." In *Greeks, Romans and Christians: Essays in Honour of Malherbe*. Edited by J. D. L. Balch, E. Ferguson and Wayne Meeks. Minneapolis: Augsburg, 1900.

Stahlin, V. G. ἀσθένεια. *TDNT* 1. Edited by Gerhard Kittel. Translated and edited by Geoffrey W. Bromiley. Grand Rapids: Eerdmans, 1964, 490–93.

Swain, John, and Sally French. "Towards an Affirmation Model of Disability." *Disability & Society* 15.4 (2000): 569–82.

Tannehill, Robert C. *Dying and Rising with Christ*. BZNW 32. Berlin: Topelmann, 1966.

Tertullian. *Against Marcion* 5. Translated and edited by Ernest Evans. Oxford: Oxford University, 1972.

Theissen, G. *The Social Setting of Pauline Christianity: Essays on Corinth*. Trans. J. H. Schulz. Philadelphia: Fortress, 1982.

———. "Social Stratification in the Corinthian Community: A Contribution to the Sociology of Early Hellenistic Christianity." In *The Social Setting of Pauline Christianity: Essays on Corinth*. Translated by J. H. Schulz. Philadelphia: Fortress, 1982, 69–120.

———. *Psychological Aspects of Pauline Theology*. Translated by J. P. Galvin. Edinburgh: T&T Clark, 1987.

Thiselton, A. C. *The First Epistle to the Corinthians: A Commentary on the Greek Text*. Grand Rapids: Eerdmans, 2000.

———. *The First Epistle to the Corinthians*. Carlisle: Paternoster, 2000.

———. "The Meaning of σάρξ in 1 Cor 5:5: A Fresh Approach in the Light of Logical and Semantic Factors," *STJ* 26 (1973): 204–28.

———. *Two Horizons: New Testament Hermeneutics and Philosophical Description with Special Reference to Heidegger, Bultmann, Gadamer, Wittgenstein*. Exeter: Paternoster, 2005.

———. "The meaning of σάρξ in 1 Cor 5:5." *SJT* 26 (1973): 204–28.

———. "Eschatology and Holy Spirit in Paul with Special Reference to 1 Cor." MTh Thesis, University of London, 1964.

Thomas, J. "παρακαλέω." *EDNT*. Edited by H. Balz and G. Schneider. 3 vols. Grand Rapids: Eerdmans, 1990–93, 23–27.

Turner, N. *Christian Words*. Edinburgh: T&T Clark, 1981.

Vanier, Jean. *Tears of Silence*. London: Darton, Longman and Todd, 1997.

———. *Community and Growth*. London: Macmillan, 1966.

Vargheese, Mathew C. "Re-visioning Ecclesia from a Disability Perspective." In *Faith and Vision: A Festschrift in Honour of Rev. Dr. T. G. Koshy*. Edited by T. M. Jose. Manakala: FTS, 2022, 165–92.

Viljoen, G. Van N. "Plato and Aristotle on the Exposure of Infants at Athens." *Acta Classica* 2 (1959): 58–69.

Weiss, J. *Earliest Christianity: A History of the Period A.D. 30–150*. Cambridge: Peter Smith, 1970.

White, H. G. Evelyn (translator). *The Homeric Hymns and Homerica*. LCL. Cambridge: Cambridge University, 1914.

Wilkenhauser, A. *Pauline Mysticism*. New York: Herder, 1960.

Wilkinson, J. *The Bible and Healing: A Medical and Theological Commentary*. Edinburgh: Handsel Press; Grand Rapids: Eerdmans, 1998.

Windisch, H. *Der zweite Korintherbrief*. Meyer K6. Göttingen: Vandenhoeck und Ruprecht, 1924.

Winter, B. W. *Philo and Paul among the Sophists*. Society for New Testament Studies Monograph Series 96. Cambridge: Cambridge University, 1997.

Witherington, B. III. *Conflict and Community in Corinth: A Socio Rhetorical Commentary on 1 and 2 Corinthians*. Grand Rapids: Eerdmans, 1995.

Wolff, C. *Der erste Brief des Paulus an die Korinther*. THKNT. Leipzig: Evangelische-Verlagsanstalt, 1996.

Yong, A. *Theology and Down Syndrome: Reimagining Disability in Late Modernity.* Waco: Baylor University, 2007.

———. *The Bible, Disability, and the Church: A New Vision of the People of God.* Grand Rapids: Eerdmans, 2011.

Yorke, Gosnell L. O. R. *The Church as the Body of Christ in the Pauline Corpus: A Re-examination.* New York: University Press of America, 1991.

Young, Frances. *Arthur's Call: A Journey of Faith in the Face of Severe Learning Disability.* London: SPCK, 2014.

——— (ed.). *Encounter with Mystery: Reflections on L'Arche and Living with Disability.* London: Darton, Longman and Todd, 1997.

———. *Face to Face: A Narrative Essay in the Theology of Suffering.* Edinburgh: T&T Clark, 1990.

———. *Brokenness and Blessing: Towards a Biblical Spirituality.* London: Darton, Longman and Todd, 2007.

Yung-Suk, Kim. *Christ's Body in Corinth: The Politics of a Metaphor.* Minneapolis: Fortress, 2008.

Zodhiates, S. *1 Corinthians.* Chattanooga: AMG, 1983.

http://www.disabled-world.com/disability/diversity.phpBrief Synopsis on 22/9/2015.

http://www.theguardian.com/commentisfree/2012/dec/13/what-is-love-five-theories on 24–8-2015.

Langham Literature and its imprints are a ministry of Langham Partnership.

Langham Partnership is a global fellowship working in pursuit of the vision God entrusted to its founder John Stott –

> *to facilitate the growth of the church in maturity and Christ-likeness through raising the standards of biblical preaching and teaching.*

Our vision is to see churches in the Majority World equipped for mission and growing to maturity in Christ through the ministry of pastors and leaders who believe, teach and live by the word of God.

Our mission is to strengthen the ministry of the word of God through:
- nurturing national movements for biblical preaching
- fostering the creation and distribution of evangelical literature
- enhancing evangelical theological education

especially in countries where churches are under-resourced.

Our ministry

Langham Preaching partners with national leaders to nurture indigenous biblical preaching movements for pastors and lay preachers all around the world. With the support of a team of trainers from many countries, a multi-level programme of seminars provides practical training, and is followed by a programme for training local facilitators. Local preachers' groups and national and regional networks ensure continuity and ongoing development, seeking to build vigorous movements committed to Bible exposition.

Langham Literature provides Majority World preachers, scholars and seminary libraries with evangelical books and electronic resources through publishing and distribution, grants and discounts. The programme also fosters the creation of indigenous evangelical books in many languages, through writer's grants, strengthening local evangelical publishing houses, and investment in major regional literature projects, such as one volume Bible commentaries like *The Africa Bible Commentary* and *The South Asia Bible Commentary*.

Langham Scholars provides financial support for evangelical doctoral students from the Majority World so that, when they return home, they may train pastors and other Christian leaders with sound, biblical and theological teaching. This programme equips those who equip others. Langham Scholars also works in partnership with Majority World seminaries in strengthening evangelical theological education. A growing number of Langham Scholars study in high quality doctoral programmes in the Majority World itself. As well as teaching the next generation of pastors, graduated Langham Scholars exercise significant influence through their writing and leadership.

To learn more about Langham Partnership and the work we do visit **langham.org**

www.ingramcontent.com/pod-product-compliance
Lightning Source LLC
Chambersburg PA
CBHW070938180426
43192CB00039B/2326